MALLORY PARK

FIFTY YEARS AT THE FRIENDLY CIRCUIT

MALLORY PARK
FIFTY YEARS AT THE FRIENDLY CIRCUIT

GARETH ROGERS

TEMPUS

First published 2006

Tempus Publishing Limited
The Mill, Brimscombe Port,
Stroud, Gloucestershire, GL5 2QG
www.tempus-publishing.com

British Library Cataloguing in Publication Data.
A catalogue record for this book is available from the British Library.

ISBN 0 7524 3851 4

Typesetting and origination by Tempus Publishing Limited
Printed in Great Britain

CONTENTS

ACKNOWLEDGEMENTS

The author would like to thank the following for their assistance with the preparation of the contents of this book and additional material: Philip Bond, Tom Cann, John Cooper, Nicki Dance, John Farnham, Julian Gerard, Martin Hadwen Motor Racing Archive, Mark Jessup, Roger Lane-Knott BDRC, Barry Lee, Helen Lovell, Wayne Lovell, David Lucas, Ron Overend, Tim Parnell, John Pearson, Wayne Pearson, David Price BARC, Brian Robinson, Phil Rogers, Michael Rutter, Sarah Sabin Renault F1, Colin Seeley, Enid Smith, Archivist BARC, Dave Stallworthy, Cynthia Wormleighton.

Photographers: Greg Brett, Gordon Bunney, Clive Challinor, Ducati, Paul Exton, John Gaisford, Ian Griffiths, Incarace, Kappa Sports Pictures, Dr Helmut Krackowizer, P. Paget, Seeley Sports, Bryan Turner, Anthony Ward, John Ward. Photograph of Barry Briggs used by permission of Robert Bamford.

DVD: The Mallory Park nostalgia DVD – seventy-five minutes of selected archive footage from the Nottingham SCC Film Unit between 1956 and 1966 plus some modern material including the Roger Clark memorial gathering.

Novel: *The Gilman File* by Bruce Widdowson. A thriller set in 1962, partly at Mallory Park and featuring the first Formula One meeting along with other historical facts about the venue. It is also produced in conjunction with the Jubilee celebrations of the circuit. Further details of both the DVD and novel from: bruce.writer@btinternet.com

BIBLIOGRAPHY

The 40th Anniversary of Mallory Park, Rennison Publications, Coventry
Mallory Park: Portrait of a Country Estate, Gareth Evans, Stowefields Publications, Stafford
Autosport
Motorcycle News
Leicestershire Life Summer 1978
The Story of Grass-Track Racing 1950-65, Robert Bamford & Dave Stallworthy, Tempus Publishing, Stroud
www.mallorypark.co.uk
www.silhouet.com/motorsport
www.btinternet.com/-john.pge/mallpk
www.lotusespritworld.co.uk
www.fi-grandprix.com
www.bbc.co.uk/dna/h2g2

FOREWORD BY JOHN SURTEES MBE

I first rode grass-track and then had my first road race at that other famous circuit – Brands Hatch – which had opened in 1950. In those days Mallory Park was a pony track, which was turned over for motorcycle grass-track events. I didn't ride in the sidecar combination with my father the first time at Mallory Park. My father, Jack, had made the switch from a 596 Norton to the Vincent HRD – the 1,000 twin – because he was the South-East agent for the marque and I was serving an apprenticeship with Vincents.

In those days Mallory Park was a big oval. It was a very fast grass-track and I think that my father set the highest speed that had been attained on a grass-track – 100mph down the back straight. So those are my first memories of Mallory Park. I have further happy memories of my Dad having a superb race there. The bike at that stage of its development had a lot of troubles and, whereas he had been a champion on the Norton, we had problems with the Vincent to start with. Mallory suited it and there it ran very well.

I wasn't the regular passenger at first but I was second mechanic and my Dad was definitely top mechanic. I didn't do any solo racing on the grass at Mallory. However, once Clive Wormleighton took over and put down the tarmac surface, with the hairpin as an addition, then I raced there with both the motorcycles and eventually the cars.

At Brands Hatch I rode a 250 Triumph but I never took that to Mallory. I do believe that I took the Vincent to Mallory Park, the grey flash. I also rode a Norton, NSU and the MV Agusta. With the new circuit you always had a challenge. Before they put the chicane in you had a very quick path down from the pits. One constant was the challenge of Gerard's corner. This was always a

John Surtees in the Race of the Year, 1958.

teaser because you arrived at it going rather quickly. The big thing was to get out of the hairpin well, so that you had the speed down from there. The hairpin, of course, was quite a different technique. It was a good passing point going into it but it was most important to get out of it quickly so as to maintain speed down past those pits. This applied to both bikes and cars.

It was surprisingly quick for a short circuit. Not just quick in a straight line – it was quick for the corners. Those corners were quick except for that one hairpin that was put in. This was one where one never concentrated on getting around the actual hairpin at a very high speed because it was quick before it and quick after it. As I said, your main preoccupation was to get into it quickly and out of it very quickly. If you concentrated on your apex speed you would probably fluff it on your way out. So you made certain that you were in the right point round the corner itself at the point of the apex to be able to get the power on early enough. Again that applied to both bikes and cars, for the lines at Mallory Park between the two wheels and the four wheels were virtually the same.

Since those days I have been up there for an historic motorcycle event in 2002. I took along a Norton and an MV Agusta. It was raining hard but all the same we took the bikes out and had a great time. I did have to adjust to a new chicane being put in, which stopped the flow of the circuit a little. However, I can well understand that much racing with today's bikes, at the speed they would come down to the pit area, had probably got excessive. All the same I must say that I enjoyed the challenge of coming over there, just about making sure that you missed the guard rails along the pit front. Of course, when I first started the guard rails weren't present. They came in at a later stage.

Safety challenges were virtually the same everywhere. You normally had circuits where you didn't have any run-off. At Mallory there was a bit of grass and the spectators would sit on the bank. The bank was there because of the excavation when the circuit was built.

With most street circuits they would put a straw bale in front of a lamppost, like they did on the Isle of Man with the motorcyclists. The same applied for cars. There wasn't the same emphasis on safety in those days. If you are talking about the cars of that period, they were considerably less safe than they are today. One of the big features that you have today is the survival cell within race cars that has been developed from Formula One. I thought guard rails were a mixed blessing for cars and they were lethal for bikes. I was very much opposed to Sir Jackie Stewart's thoughts on that. I was on the opposite side – not for the first time with Sir Jackie! Where the big safety factors came in was with the big increase in funds that came from television and other ancillaries. This allowed the adoption of some space technology and the creation of that safety cell in a modern chassis in formula racing.

Mallory Park had its dangers but its record has been relatively good, as such. It's a short circuit, a challenging circuit and a quick circuit. Luckily there have not been too many attempts to put chicanes in. I can well understand some people saying that Gerard's is too fast and let's slow it down. So far it remains pure. The fact remains that Gerard's is a bit of a teaser. You can always have the situation with Gerard's that you are always open to competitors with more heroics and a little less brain 'doing their thing' where they may come into the corner that much quicker. By the time that they are halfway through they are in trouble. In the meantime they have spoilt your line. The situation, if possible, is to steer clear of others on somewhere like Gerard's. You want to get out and away. Luckily, I was very adept at being able to get off the line quickly so I didn't really encounter any major problems. That was in the days of a push and bump start.

Mallory Park is a challenge and that's what it should be. We are very fortunate in this country to have some super circuits. I remember visiting the circuits with my father beforehand and then coming onto them myself. The first circuit that I ever saw was the old mountain road race circuit at Cadwell Park. That, in its own way, had tremendous character. Then the rest of the circuits came along. Against that you have the Silverstones, the Aintrees, the Snettertons – places that were originally airfields. As such they have a certain standard of racing but not the character. Mallory is also a natural grandstand. This is the beauty. Brands

Hatch and Mallory Park between them have the better viewing for spectators. The fact remains that if you stand up on the bank at Mallory you see exactly what the racers are doing, the lines and flow. The fans are not peering over – they are looking down. The length of Mallory means that you see a lot of the action. They are not disappearing out into the country. There is very much a place in motor sport for these short circuits. What I find amazing is that with the benefit of all these superb circuits like Mallory Park we have found it so difficult to produce a new Motorcycling World Champion – and a new Formula One World Champion for that matter. The circuits that we have in Britain are wonderful for developing skills.

I think that we are partly to blame for it ourselves. Often we have gone along and pumped people up as champions of this and champions of that – for example, champion of Mallory or champion of Brands – so that they think they have arrived and so never go for the ultimate challenge.

Mallory Park was a very important part of my own development and history as I did enjoy success there on both two and four wheels. The big MV I took there was not the finest type of machine for this sort of circuit. It needed a lot of physical effort because of the high centre of gravity. Mallory is a track where you must come as one with your machine, whether it happens to be a two-wheel or a four-wheel. You will get away with many things on many circuits. You don't take liberties with Mallory because you can hurt yourself. That in turn is an important factor. I think that the Isle of Man has made many mistakes making the place more dangerous because they have taken the apparent danger out of it by straightening out sections of road. As a consequence people tend to treat it with less respect at times than it deserves. Mallory you can never treat with less respect. It is somewhere that keeps you busy. It has got this variation of fast and the odd slow corner. Just the one where, let's face it, if anyone is going to do it wrongly it will be on the slowest part of the circuit. The rest of it requires precision and, although you can take more than one line, there are basically ways to ride it and ways not to ride it to ensure that you get into these quick ones and you get out of them. It's all interdependent. The Esses, as such, they are more like an exercise where you have to flick the machine over from one side to another. The teaser, generally, where races will be won, would be Gerard's.

The cars I competed in were Formula One, although in a Tasman form with a 2.7 litre engine. This was a Lola. I also raced a Formula Two car, again a Lola, in which I was called 'The Master of Mallory' in one press account. The F1 Lola was a car that I helped create with the support of Yeoman Credit, the Samengo-Turner brothers and Reg Parnell. In its first year we nearly won a Grand Prix with it but I got pipped in Germany. We finished the World Championship in front of both Ferrari and Porsche. That was 1962. It was a tremendous first year for a debut Formula One team. We then put a 2.7 Climax Tasman engine in it. They informed me that there was a 1,000 guineas race at Mallory Park. So I said, 'Let's take it there.' I went there and it was a good field. It just went away. That was a car that had come good at the end of the year. So I finished the season on a good note and was signed up by Ferrari virtually after that race. The rest is history, as they say. That race at Mallory was before we went off for the Tasman winter series. Having turned the car from 1.5 litres to the other, I won at Lakeside and also at Longford in Tasmania. So Mallory Park had been my last European appearance in that car because I was joining Ferrari.

It was a good period to be racing. A lot depended on equipment, obviously, and as always. With Lola we had an uphill struggle against the established teams like Coopers and Lotus, plus Ferrari and Porsche. Despite a first-year effort it would have been nice to win the odd Grand Prix that year. We came close to it but there were silly little problems. It was pleasing to finish the home season with a nice win at Mallory and mix and mingle with the British enthusiasts – there was a lot of enthusiasm, and still is – for they could see the cars and drivers at

The era of 'mix and mingle'.

these events, something that doesn't happen these days. They would have been able to come down the paddock, wander around and look at the cars and talk to the drivers. The nearest situation that you have today is what I'm involved in now, which is the A1 series. In those days it had not developed into the enormous business that you have today. In many ways it is a little disjointed because what you have is Formula One, which has developed on the back of television and universal support, and projects itself to the world as motor sport. Of course, there is an awful lot of motor sport other than Formula One. Unfortunately, the fact that Formula One has relied on generating so much income has its effect on making it more difficult for everything else that is below it. Even starting with a kart is more costly because of what people expect relative to an involvement with motor sport. This is a great shame, frankly. The current Formula One drivers have grown up in a different era. I'm seeing in A1 GP at the moment a number of youngsters who will always be aspiring to be in Formula One but who are showing their abilities, trying to demonstrate to the world that they not only represent their country – within the country's car that they are racing – but also they are demonstrating their ability on global television. You can see some inspirational passing movements in this formula. None of them are being paid a fortune. In some cases they are being paid nothing but prize money if they happen to win. However, they are all at that stage of life where they are competing for the sake of competing. I'm afraid that you tend to find that there are a percentage of those who are in Formula One who frankly shouldn't be there. I am not talking about Michael Schumacher who, despite everything, remains a competitor. Despite all the money, despite all the glory, he is an optimum example of a competitor but there are others who shouldn't be there. None of the people who lined up against me you would treat as faint-hearted. They would all have a go, irrespective of the conditions. Also they had one thing – they had their hearts in motor sport. They loved it. More so than one or two who were to follow.

As for conviviality at Mallory Park – I was not the most social person. I can't pretend to have been but Clive Wormleighton always put on a decent function at the clubhouse. One felt part of the scene. It was always an enjoyable place to be because you actually felt as if you were wanted, which is rather nice. He created, I think, quite a good support because the trade liked going there as they were well accommodated and looked after. There was a genuinely good atmosphere. Clive was quite a character. He was also very receptive to ideas. Chris Meek, who owns it now, is that way. Chris is damn genuine at heart. He hasn't got a lot of time for much of the hypocrisy that goes around any sport and motor sport is no exception. Chris is also a good businessman and Mallory Park is a little jewel in its own way.

To have a statue unveiled of me was rather a strange phenomenon. Suddenly Chris came to me and said, 'We are going to build a statue of you there.' He continued, 'There should be one. I don't know why yours wasn't there first.' I replied, 'Well, that's not up to me.' I duly went up. It was very nice. Mr Kawamoto, the ex-president of Honda, with his colleagues, came to the opening. A lot of my old friends came together for the occasion. It brought back memories of my winning the motorcycle 'Race of the Year' when I was twenty-two years old, plus my four-wheel career developing largely out of my time in Formula Two at the circuit.

I am pleased that Chris Meek still owns it and that BARC have the new lease. They can maintain the spirit that existed at Mallory. Luckily the circuit did not fall into other hands. It's important not to make it a Silverstone or a Thruxton or anything else. Mallory is Mallory. So treat Mallory as it is. It has got its own character as a circuit. You can liken this corner or that to somewhere else but luckily it's not just a flat type of challenge. You have got the character where you can have some extremely good racing but there is a warmth about Mallory and that normally includes both competitors and spectators.

I remain active. We were never paid enough not to remain active. That's only an excuse – actually I love it as well. The fact remains that I've always said that one of the important factors, which so many sportsmen tend to forget, is that we

Japanese visitors at John Surtees' unveiling.

Henry Surtees, winner, Junior Gearbox Championship, 2005.

got involved in the sports of our choosing because of an emotional involvement. The fact that you actually get paid is a privilege. It shouldn't overcome the emotional involvement.

Today I am involved in the A1 series and officially fronting up the British team. We have also assisted in setting up the Canadian team. It's an interesting concept with interesting drivers.

I am looking forward to taking my son Henry up to Mallory Park. Henry is just turning over to cars. In 2005 he won the Junior Gearbox Championship in karting. He was fifteen in February 2006. I want to take him testing. That would be very appropriate as a family and he can learn something.

Meanwhile, what I am impressing on Henry is that we don't talk Formula One and we don't talk about it being his future. We talk about racing being his present because it has to take second place to school. There is no place in this life for a stupid racing driver – if you choose to be a racing driver. It is better to have backup as well. So you can't neglect school but first and foremost it has to come from within. You have got to do it because it gives you pleasure.

When he won the Junior Gearbox Championship that was a great delight to me because he is a very sturdily built lad so he is running with a penalty of about seven kilos. Henry is over the weight limit. That is something that has caused me to make the decision of where we went from here. So we put him in a little junior Ginetta and he went out and got third place in his first race and fourth place in his second at Silverstone. I then dropped him in at the deep end entirely by hiring a T-car. That was less than successful. We had a lot of problems with the set-up of the car, which at that stage he shouldn't have had. At the same time it was a useful lesson for him. Then he went off to Silverstone to take part in a shoot-out with some of his current competitors and was fastest in the car-driving section. So that was very pleasing.

I keep telling myself that I must stand well back but I find that very difficult to do. I'm afraid that it's not the easiest situation for him in the world. He has been very much targeted in his karting because of his surname. It is an unfortunate factor but that is life. That in turn has helped develop his strength of character. I've said to him that I am not going to supply all the enthusiasm. Whatever he chooses – playing rugby is another love of his – I will support him. So that is where we are at the moment in 2006 with Mallory Park as our test bed. His grandfather would surely approve!

FOREWORD BY
CHRIS MEEK

When Mallory was purchased, including the estate, in 1983, I cemented a long relationship with the circuit that went back to the 1950s. My first race was in 1957 with my first win on Whit Monday 1959 in an Elva Courier. The last race I won there was in 1983. During that time I experienced the widest spectrum of emotions, highlights and disappointments but one thing is for certain – it was always exciting and never dull on what has always been my favourite circuit.

We have come a long way since those first days, with development accelerating since 1983 and providing better and better facilities. To date this is represented by the new race control, hospitality suite and pit building, along with a new medical centre, the Meek Suite and many other improvements.

It always has been and still is a high-speed circuit demanding expertise and skill of the highest order and incorporating the unique Gerard's curve.

From managing a third place in the 1957 race driving a Lotus Mk VIII side-valve (1,172cc) I went on over the years with a procession of wins and lap records in the following classes: Sports, GT, cars, single seaters and saloons with first places in such as Elvas, Ginettas, De Tomaso, Lotus, MG, Ford, TVR, Panther and Titan.

As to the future, I can see further extensions to the race control/pits complex, revised pit access and improved paddock area and a possible extension to the circuit itself. The activities outside the circuit will continue to expand, including the extensive restoration of the Coach House and its surroundings, together with the creation of the Mallory Park centre plus new workshops to facilitate those associated with the circuit and estate, motorcycle trials course, speedway track and corporate-sponsored activities.

Left: Hailwood Hospitality Suite.

Below: Race control.

Opposite above: The Meek Suite.

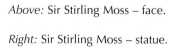

Above: Sir Stirling Moss – face.

Right: Sir Stirling Moss – statue.

Chris Meek.

We try to put a little bit into the sport by honouring our greatest British heroes through the creation of life-size bronze statues celebrating the achievements of John Surtees, Jim Clark, Mike Hailwood, Roger Clark and Colin Chapman. In June 2006 there will be an unveiling of a statue of Sir Stirling Moss.

Having been the owner of Mallory Park longer than any of those previously – for some twenty-three years – I look forward to the future as owner for another twenty-three years!

PROLOGUE:
THE MISTS OF TIME

The history of Mallory Park goes back into the mists of time from the Roman road that passed through the estate and its mention in the Domesday book. In its early days it was associated with Hugh De Grentemaisnk, a companion of William the Conqueror. He was the largest landowner and the most powerful feudal lord in the country.

The name of Mallory appears in the middle of the twelfth century. The Mallorys were certainly fighting men and must have arrived with an invading force at some time. They fraternised on equal terms with the leading Norman families, inter-marrying with them and holding some of their own manors 'of the King in Chief'. After the time of King Stephen (1133-1154) the Mallory family is recorded as holding manors and land in many counties, not only Leicestershire.

In the Domesday survey the township is called Cherchebi but it was already known as Kirkby Mallory when Geoffrey Mallory was Lord of the Manor in the time of King Stephen and into the reign of Henry II (1154-1189). There was a confirmation of arms by 1569. Thomas Mallory, the eldest son of Geoffrey had 'a lion rampant gules collared argent' – a lion without a forked tail, it seems. These arms suggest that the Mallory lion was single-tailed when first granted and that Kirkby Mallory, although the senior branch, did not receive a coat of arms until the practice of differencing by a forked tail was adopted. The Mallory colours of gold and scarlet may indicate royal service at some time, since these reflect the arms of England. The family lived in a fortified manor house situated just north of the present racing circuit.

The greatest honour that may be claimed by the Mallory family is that of being direct ancestors of the late Queen Mother, the Lady Elizabeth Bowes-Lyon and

Kirkby Hall.

consequently of the reigning British Royal Family. Dorothy Mallory, daughter of Sir William Mallory, married Sir George Bowes of Streatlam, Durham in 1529.

The family flourished until the late 1600s. Then, in each house, either the male line failed or misfortune required them to sell their properties. It was about this time that many Mallorys emigrated to America. Following a series of owners of the 200-acre estate, the property was acquired by the Noel family for the next 370 years. The Noels were subsequently ennobled as the Wentworths. Lord Byron, the poet, married into the Wentworth family and on the rare occasions that he visited Mallory Park it is said that he worked under the outstanding Lebanon Cedar Tree that still stands in the grounds.

Kirkby Mallory was, for most of the nineteenth century, occupied by the family of Baroness De Clifford. Its ownership had passed through the marriage of Lady Byron's daughter, to the Earl of Lovelace. The Lovelace family disposed of it in 1921. The estate was bought by the sitting tenant, Mr H.C. Hartley, who had lived there since the 1890s. Following his death in 1941 there were a variety of owners.

With a natural basin allowing an ideal viewing venue, a pony trotting track was planned. Construction work first started in the 1940s. Marsh ground was drained

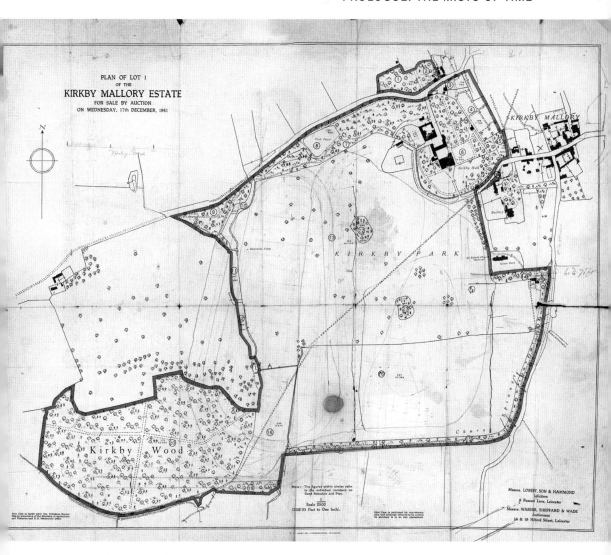

The 1941 estate plan.

and a small strip of Kirkby Wood was cleared to accommodate the track. However, the bulk of the mature trees had been felled earlier under the instruction of the 'War Agricultural Committee' as a contribution towards the war effort.

The 1,660-yard oval grass track was eventually completed in the late 1940s with a judges' box erected and starting gates in position. Then, without warning, the Kirkby Mallory Racing Association, together with the Shirley Racecourse and other associated companies, was forced to cease trading when the parent company the Pony Turf Club went into liquidation. The Leicester Query Club

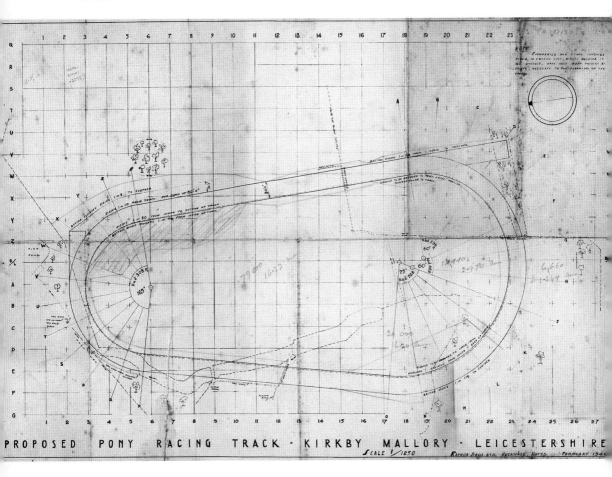

PROPOSED PONY RACING TRACK · KIRKBY MALLORY · LEICESTERSHIRE

Pony-trotting track plans.

then rented the track to put on motorcycle events from 1949 until 1954. The highlights were the staging of the National Grass-Track Racing Championships, the first being held in September 1951. Interestingly, a Mr Murray Walker was often the public address announcer.

The eighteenth-century hall, following occupation by the Army during the Second World War, was demolished in 1952 although the coach house and stable block were left standing. These buildings eventually became the circuit offices, workshops and the Coach House hotel, pub and restaurant.

During May 1953 the whole estate, consisting of over 300 acres, was put up for auction and purchased by a Mr H.W. Moult of Derby, who wanted to utilise the unused pony track for horse racing, but his plans never materialised. In 1955 the estate was purchased by Clive Wormleighton from East Shilton – a local builder and, crucially, a motor sport enthusiast. The magic of Mallory was about to unfold!

" The Companies Act, 1929."

COMPANY LIMITED BY SHARES.

Memorandum of Association

OF

Kirkby Mallory Racecourse Company,
LIMITED.

1. The Name of the Company is " KIRKBY MALLORY RACECOURSE COMPANY, LIMITED."

2. The Registered Office of the Company will be situate in England.

3. The Objects for which the Company is established are—

(A) To carry on the business of a Racecourse Company in all its branches, and in particular to purchase, take on lease, or otherwise acquire, and prepare any lands for the running of horse or pony races, steeplechases, or races of any other kind, and for any kind of athletic sports and for playing thereon games of cricket, polo, golf, croquet, lawn tennis, bowls, or any other kind of amusement, recreation, sport, or entertainment, and to construct grand or other stands, booths, stables for horses and other animals, kennels, totalisators, refreshment rooms, concert halls, and other erections, buildings, and conveniences whether of a permanent or temporary nature, which may seem directly or indirectly conducive to the Company's objects, and to conduct, hold, and promote race meetings and athletic sports, polo, lawn tennis, and other matches, agricultural, horse, flower, and other shows and exhibitions, and otherwise utilise the Company's property and rights in any way which may seem desirable, and to give and contribute towards prizes, cups, stakes, and other rewards.

(B) To establish any clubs, hotels, or other conveniences in connection with the Company's property.

(C) To carry on the business of Hotel, Restaurant, Tavern, Café, and Refreshment Room Keepers, Licensed Victuallers, Refreshment Purveyors, Wine, Beer, and Spirit Merchants, Tobacconists, Manufacturers of and Dealers in Aerated, Mineral and Artificial Waters, Ballroom Proprietors, Caterers for Public Amusements generally, Coach, Cab, Carriage, and Motor Proprietors, Garage Proprietors, Livery Stable Keepers, Farmers, Stud Farmers, Dairymen, Market Gardeners, Timber Merchants, Growers, and Fellers, and Breeders of and Dealers in Horses and other Animals.

Memorandum of Association, Kirkby Racecourse Co.

81488

29

A MAN OF VISION

Despite the fact that planning permission had been granted in 1954 to develop parts of the estate for residential purposes, Clive Wormleighton's sights were not on housing but on a motor racing circuit. This is confirmed by his widow, Cynthia: 'Clive had done a lot of building in the area and was offered the Kirkby Mallory Estate. I'm pretty sure at the time that there was planning permission for up to twenty properties of an acre each and it would have been an attractive site. However, at the time the Leicester Query Motorcycle Club were quite active holding grass-track meetings and they had been using it as a venue for grass-track racing. It was just the oval as we know it today. He came and had a look. Motorcycle racing at that time was in its full swing. It gave him the vision of extending the track with a hairpin. He put a few feelers out for people who were interested, though some thought it would never get off the ground. Before the Second World War he used to go to Donington. He didn't marshal at races or anything like that. He was a spectator. Clive was a sportsman and he liked all sports, including motor sport – especially motorcycling as he had ridden a motorcycle in his younger days.

'When he came to Mallory he thought that the spectator potential was wonderful. Planning permission for the circuit was never ever easy. Clive did make the effort to go around all the houses in the village asking if they had any objections. Then there was quite a delay and he got the local Member of Parliament involved – Mr Arthur Allen, a Labour MP. They had kept us waiting quite some time and we did go up to London to find out what was going on. Eventually planning permission was granted. Noise is always an issue but I don't

Clive Wormleighton (right) with Mr Ray Smith (Solo champion, left) and Mr John Burton (Scrambles champion, centre).

think many of the neighbourhood quite realised that. So those Friday nights knocking on the door and consulting did pay off, though many didn't quite realise what it would entail.

'He gave his all to the project. Clive was very go-ahead. He had vision and he was determined. If he set his mind on something he wouldn't change it.'

Work started in 1956 on redesigning the circuit. The first major project was to construct a hard racing surface in place of the existing turf. The second was to extend the track by adding that hairpin bend at the northerly end of the circuit. This increased the length from just under a mile to 1.35 miles. The work was overseen by Clive Wormleighton's foreman Jack Perridge, who lived locally. An extension to the original oval embraced a well-banked right-hand hairpin. This climbed gently away from the old circuit, returning at a higher level to rejoin the starting straight in a downhill left-hand sweep. This became known as 'Shaw's Corner' after Jack Shaw, the late secretary of the Leicester Query Club.

Cynthia reminds us of the build-up to the circuit actually staging races: 'Come the launch Bob Gerard and Maurice Cann were involved. Bob Gerard lived at

The original circuit.

The launch by Bob Gerard and Maurice Cann.

Markfield, about eight miles way. Maurice Cann lived at Countersthorpe. Bob Gerard had a motor car garage in Leicester. Maurice Cann had a motorcycle business and garage in Leicester. They had strong local links and both were very good at their sport. Bob had been quite a famous personality, as indeed had Maurice Cann. Bob Gerard was a charming person and we were friendly with Maurice Cann. They were both interested and delighted with the possibility of a racing circuit in proximity.'

Bob McIntyre.

Maurice Cann on his way to winning the 1947 250cc Ulster Cup.

Above: Bob Gerard, pre-war.

Right: Bob Gerard with victory laurel.

Maurice Cann – winner of the 1948 250cc TT.

Bob's nephew, Julian, recalls the career and involvement at Mallory Park of Frederick Robert Gerard, who began racing in a Riley in 1933: 'During the Second World War he bought an ex-Johnny Wakefield BRA R14 off Reg Parnell, who was storing it for the Wakefield family. Johnny Wakefield was killed in the war. Bob was based at Desford Aerodrome during the war in the Home Guard, so he was able to keep working on the cars throughout the war. When he started racing again after the war he was quite well prepared, hence his good results. Racing was very club-biased, and mainly sports cars. He did hill climbs as well. I was a lad of ten when Mallory opened. Bob was delighted. I think that he officially opened it with a Cooper Bristol. BRAs had gone by then. By 1956 he had a lot of competitive experience. He had raced at Grand Prix level; he was third in 1947 at Silverstone and second in 1948. When Mallory came along he was well-known in British motor sport and he knew Clive Wormleighton. They got on well. So it was natural for him to do the opening and a bonus to have a corner named after him. Of course he then raced there and by the 1970s the track was staging the Bob Gerard Trophy. He retired from racing in 1964 but he did his last race at Mallory Park in a Cooper BMC Formula Junior.'

Racing contemporary Peter Tinnion recalls two facets of Maurice Cann: 'Apparently he won the race in the Isle of Man in 1947 but they gave the victory to another rider, Austin Monks. In those days the timing was just on stop watches. Years later the other rider admitted it.

'I also remember Maurice having to warm his Castrol R, which was like chewing gum, on a primer stove. You can't believe it, can you? These riders today don't know what it is all about.'

The official opening took place on Wednesday 26 April 1956. Under the headline 'Fastest small track in the country: Gerard's Mallory Park verdict' came the following report from *Autosport* magazine: 'Lapping at speeds well in excess of 80 miles per hour, international racing driver Bob Gerard and leading motorcyclist Maurice Cann signalled the return of top-class speed events to Leicestershire for the first time since Donington Park closed in 1939 at the official opening of the new Mallory Park track today.

'Constructed at a cost of £60,000 by local builder Mr T. Clive Wormleighton, this short but tricky 1.35-mile circuit will offer drivers both speed and a test of their nerve and skill. Oval shaped, it has a hairpin bend – Shaw's Corner – at one end with a deceptive curve, where races may be won or lost, at the other.

'Laps of honour were reeled off by Bob Gerard in a Cooper Bristol and Manx GP winner Maurice Cann on a Moto Guzzi. Bob Gerard achieved a lap of 81mph. Thanks to his advice and input during the track's development plus his international achievements from his roots as a local man, a bend at the circuit was named in his honour.'

On the following Saturday, 29 April, there was a track practice that was again attended by an *Autosport* reporter: 'Between fifty and sixty riders turned out last Saturday for an informal try-out of the new 1.35-mile Kirkby Mallory track, organised by the Leicester Query Club. Not its baptism, of course…

'Now it is complete to the last flagpole, and the smoothly laid, metalled surface promises to give superlative tyre adhesion, even in the wet.

'After the starting straight comes a long, wide-radiused right-hand curve, which many riders found the trickiest section since the line is not readily apparent. There follows the back straight and another curve from which a spur runs tangentially to Shaw's Corner, a hairpin where the course doubles back on itself to a left-hand down-hill sweep named Devil's Elbow, and so back into the starting straight at the end of which speeds of up to 115mph were being reached.

'The try-out augured well for the track's success, several riders putting up excellent times, despite their short acquaintance with it.'

Among those who took part that day was Peter Tinnion, but his experience was less cosy than the perspective of the reporter. Peter, from Derby, was a competitive racer by the time that Mallory opened, having ridden at Senior Clubman's level at the Isle of Man since 1952: 'When Mallory came along that was a bonus. Before the track opened they had this practice to find out what riders thought of it. The circuit was very smooth because of Clive Wormleighton's building background but it was ideal for motor cars. You were okay on the straights but once you got on the bends – and bear in mind in those years, long before John Cooper rode, the tyres were just like road tyres with a straight edge – you would go so far and there's no tread. When John developed those 'V' tyres with Dunlop you pretty well had a full tread so you could hang out of the saddle – but you couldn't then. That practice day at Mallory I rode a Gold Star and a 250 Velocette that we made up with the spring frame. As I recall there were twenty-five or thirty riders trying out on the track that day. We were all decent racers and knew where we were going. At the time I thought that the circuit was too smooth, although I had reasonable success with it. I did like granite chips like the Isle of Man. If it rained there then you were racing on sandpaper. It was great even with the tyres in those days.

'As for the shape of the Mallory circuit – the Esses bends were the worst for me. Other than that it wasn't truly a road circuit as I knew it. After the war there were lots of aerodrome circuits. They were just concrete and we didn't know any better. So you think that's as good as it gets. I liked Cadwell Park and Scarborough, which were road circuits.

'After that first practice I had the opportunity to race at Mallory. I did win one or two heats – nothing great. Now I look back on those days and realise how wonderful they were. Freedom and a good social life. The practice was very easy going. There wasn't the officialdom that you have today. It was less regulated. Dealing with the feedback from riders was all very friendly. It wasn't so serious. I remember Clive Wormleighton that day. He wasn't anonymous and he did move around to speak to people.'

The first race meeting took place on Sunday 13 May to a *Motorcycling* magazine heading of: 'Curtain up at Kirkby Mallory: Packed programme at the new Leicestershire circuit.' The article read: 'In brilliant sunshine, a crowd estimated at well over 20,000 thronged the natural grandstands at Kirkby Mallory, Leicestershire, last Sunday, for the inaugural meeting of this latest addition to the road-racers repertoire. And just as crowded was the programme provided by the Leicester Query Motorcycle Club – 248 riders competing in a total of twenty-nine short events, which took nearly seven and a half hours to complete.

'Though this may indicate that the club has not yet achieved a complete transition from grass-track to road-race technique, the spectators showed no sign of dissatisfaction, almost all staying to the very end. They were rewarded with

Maurice Cann starts the first motorcycle meeting, 13 May 1956.

the two hardest-fought and most thrilling races of the day, the 1,000cc sidecar handicap in which Pip Harris (449 Norton) pushed the lap record for "chairs" to within a fraction of 80mph and the 500cc solo final, when G.T. Salt (George), also on a Norton, notched the absolute fastest at 84.08mph.

'Several spectacular accidents occurred but none were serious and, if anything, they served to indicate the safety of the track and spectator protection. In the third 1,000cc sidecar heat, C.H.R. Warner (988 Vincent) lost tyre adhesion entering the Esses and ran full tilt into the earth bank with extensive damage to his previously immaculate streamlining, and, on the left-hand Devil's Elbow, A. Ellis looped his Norton outfit in the third sidecar handicap, unaware, too late, of the fact that he had shed his passenger at Shaw's Corner.'

The first car meeting was held on the following Whit Monday, 21 May. Under the heading 'Mallory Park overture – Successful first race meeting at new 1.4 mile Leicestershire road circuit', the *Autosport* magazine reported that: 'Under glorious weather conditions, the first car meeting, well organised by the Nottingham Sports Car Club, took place on Whit Monday at Mallory Park, the new Midland road circuit near Leicester.

'This track, measuring some 1.4 miles of new-laid tarmac is practically oval-shaped with an ancillary rising loop to a rather acute hairpin. Racing was watched by a very large crowd of spectators who, aided by a natural bank opposite the main straight, could follow the cars some two-thirds of the way round.

'It is obvious that a great deal of thought and money has been put into this project. The course is smooth, level and perfectly marked with permanent buildings, which include a most elaborate raised press box, situated above and opposite the start area. It is understood that grandstands will be erected in time for the August meeting. Spectator control was excellent; in fact the only suggestion for improvement would be to widen the rather acute rising hairpin at Shaw's Corner, which rather penalises any car that has not too generous a lock.

'The meeting started with a combined seven-lap scratch race for the 750cc and 1,172cc formula sports cars, the former being won by D. Rees (Austin) at 64.7mph, with Anstice Brown (Lotus) taking the larger class at 70.08mph. What might have been a nasty incident occurred on lap seven, when Jack French's Austin, driven by Arthur Mallock, appeared to turn into the pit area, momentarily unsighting P.A. Cross, who demolished the pits entrance sign – luckily without injury.'

On 7 July the British Racing and Sports Car Club ran their first meeting at Mallory. Among the entrants were Graham Hill, Colin Chapman and Bob Gerard. Also entered was Don Truman, who eventually became the BRSCC'S clerk of the course at Mallory and of whom we shall hear more later. So Bob Gerard began to actually compete on the circuit that he helped launch and where a corner was named in his honour. His involvement led to happy memories for young Julian Gerard: 'I would have first come to Mallory Park in 1957 or 1958. My father used to bring me to watch. It was the best viewing arena for motor racing in the country. We stood at Devil's Elbow. It was a bond to watch a member of the family and Bob was always at the front. He was a very quick, very tidy, very smooth driver. Yet he didn't look quick – he was deceptively good. Bob drove Turner sports cars as well – and had titanic battles with various Austin Healy Sprites. He was always smooth while the Sprites were all over the place.

'Bob was still competing with drivers who went on to achieve greatness in the sport. He was a contemporary of Stirling Moss and actually drove Stirling's 250 at Charterhall. He apparently got on very well with it. That was the only time he drove a foreign car. Bob was totally pro-British. As a person, Bob was quite shy. He didn't mix with the lads. He kept himself to himself. He wasn't aloof, however. He wasn't cold if you got him talking about engineering. He was a brilliant engineer and that's where he found the speeds for the cars. He spent a lot of time on the cars. He had a marvellous engineering facility at Abbey Lane in Leicester. His company was the only one in the world allowed to rebuild Gardener diesel engines under licence and they went all round the world in trawlers and all sorts. In the height of the racing days the Gardeners were pushed to one side – the dynos were full of Bristol engines, ERAs and all sorts. Everything went on the dynos down to little Sprite engines. All his cars were super-quick.

'Away from my memories of him as a consistent performer around Mallory Park, I did eventually drive there myself. As a tutor he was brilliant. You could cut part of your learning curve but he would tell you if you had done wrong in no uncertain terms. As for having a bend named after him – he never shouted about it. He used to giggle that it used to catch people out. "Well, it would!" he uttered. It was like a double corner really – you had to treat it as two corners and to go around there quickly.'

Meanwhile, Clive Wormleighton had to make business decisions about the circuit's diary, as Cynthia Wormleighton recalls: 'In the early days he didn't see that at this stage an event could be held every week, as it is now. In fact the first year we didn't have too many planned meetings, half motorcycling, half cars. We had one or two "bad weather" days. So we thought, well, the next year you are sure to get some "bad weather meetings". You can ten meetings and every one of them could be fine, or you could have twenty and every one of them could be wet. After a year or two he thought, why not have a few meetings and make them really good ones? He felt that if you could go every week or every other week there wouldn't be the thrill or the atmosphere of the odd occasion. Now if it were once a month it would be full. So he tried to make it alternate between cars and motorcycles. On Bank Holidays – that was Easter Monday, Whit Monday and August Bank Holiday, the first Monday in August in those days – he did, in fact, always have a car meeting. They were very popular but so was motorcycling. They were equally popular. I wouldn't say one or the other. Both had their own following.

'He introduced the Post-TT in June and then the Race of the Year – it was his idea for the Race of the Year.

'We did do the Boxing Day meeting and only did it a couple of times because in the run-up to Christmas you had to get matters started again. It did tend to spoil your Christmas festivities. You could do all those preparations and on that day there could be a frost or a fog.

'The money that he made, he did plough it back. It was a gamble. Looking back now you could think that it wasn't. We didn't know then. Of course, being a builder – although contractors laid the tarmac – he knew what was involved as he had developed estates on which there were roads. He could supervise matters. He wanted to get the circuit correct from the start. As a young man he would have liked to be an architect. In those days his parents would have had to pay a premium and he would have had to work for nothing. His parents couldn't

PROGRAMME for 1958

March 23rd
Leicester Query Club.   Motorcycle racing.

April 7th (Easter Monday)
Nottingham Sports Car Club.   Motor Car racing—National Meeting.

April 12th
Coventry Cycling Club.   Cycle racing.

April 13th
Nottingham Tornado Club.   Motorcycle racing.

May 11th
B.R.S.C.C.   Motor car racing—National Meeting.

May 26th (Whit Monday)
N.S.C.C.   Car racing—National Meeting.

June 8th
A.C.U. Midlands Centre.   Motorcycle racing—National Meeting.

July 13th
Leicester Query Club.   Motorcycle racing.

August 4th (August Monday)
N.S.C.C.   Motor car racing—National Meeting.

September 7th
Nottingham Tornado Club.   Motorcycle racing.

October 5th
Nottingham Tornado Club.   Motorcycle racing (Novices).

The programme of events for 1958.

afford one or the other. So he became an apprentice carpenter and at twenty-one, after his apprenticeship, he started his own building business. At Mallory he combined an architect's mind with his building skills. Another interesting point about Clive was that once he had done something he was always ready to move on. He always had his mind to the future and another challenge.

'We had a campaign run against us by the Lord's Day Observance Society but we overcame that by charging for the car and not admission, a car park fee to meet the legal restraints. That opposition fizzled out after a time. They gave up the ghost. Whatever you try to do you will get objections. We did try and tie in with the church services if it was a Sunday, particularly because of its proximity. Again, we tried to help the village. We started a bowling club on a bowling green, which brought some of them in. We held an annual tea party and a Christmas

Waterskiing.

do for the old folk. Clive didn't have quite the good relationship that Edwina Overend had in subsequent years. She joined in more activities.'

Cynthia refers to reinvestment and during the winter of 1957-58 the very narrow hairpin at Shaw's was widened up to twenty feet and the large and rather dangerous tree guarding Shaw's exit was removed. Also, within the inner area of the track one small and one large lake was created, the smaller for fishing and the larger for fishing, sailing, motor boats and water sports. The project manager was John Coe: 'I served my time with Clive in the building trade from 1949. He came to me and said that he had an interesting job for me – at Mallory Park. So we moved the workshop at Earl Shilton and all the machinery en bloc from there to Mallory, which helped when you are working at a place like that. It was ideal. It was handy really as we had all the kit. Initially I worked on improvements such as the press box and the commentary box from which Murray Walker worked at the motorcycle races.

'We had seven experienced builders on site – bricklayers, plumbers etc. It made it more cost-effective for Clive, who had made a significant investment.

'Before I was given the task of putting the lakes in, what we had was a very wet, desolate piece of ground in the middle of the circuit. Nothing had been done by the people who had put the pony track in. It had all been left overgrown and the brook that came through the centre was only two feet wide. It ran straight through and under the track and out the other side in the old stream path. Then we had this idea that we should make it look better with a lake in the middle. So that's what we did. We put a pier on the end of Gerard's bend. We piped it and put a valve in. Then we turned the valve on. It didn't take that long, about a couple of months to fill. Then we had a leak – a hole appeared at the side of the pipe – and it emptied within a week. Clive's reaction wasn't very good! What we did was to reinforce the bank with polythene then put fondue concrete down – quick-setting stuff on the part where the pressure was at Gerard's Corner on the bend. In no time it filled back up. The lake was Clive's concept and it certainly adds to the presentation of the circuit. We did another lake further on towards the Esses. It all makes Mallory rather distinctive.

'Even today the basics of the original circuit are still there. I can obviously see the changes. The commentary box and the control centre are superb. We just knocked something up that did the job at the time. Quite a transition!'

The following winter saw two further developments. A new control tower was built and up at Shaw's a large open stand, high on pylons, was erected. It was positioned so that spectators were able to see clearly both the approach and exit of the spectacular hairpin.

The lake.

One sight that nobody wanted to see was a fatality. The first at Mallory Park occurred in 1959, as reported by the Gazette of the British Automobile Racing Club (BARC): 'The fifth Mallory Park members' meeting on 19 September was marred by a fatal accident in the first race, which cast a cloud of depression over the whole meeting and took pleasure out of some good racing. On the second lap of the 500cc scratch race there was a collision between the Coopers of Don Parker, who had made an extremely slow start and was fast working his way through the small field, and Peter Mutton, who was then lying fourth. Parker was able to crawl to the verge from the wreckage that littered the track, but Mutton was killed.'

There were other challenges for Clive and Cythia too as the circuit established itself: 'In our early days at Mallory doubt was expressed about whether we would attract the top stars. Brands Hatch was that much longer. Goodwood was very much favoured in motor sport circles. Snetterton had a length advantage for motorcyclists. However, with Clive putting up good prize money it did attract them. Some venues didn't want us to give too much prize money. Whether it was about racers taking too many risks I don't know. Perhaps it was having to match the prize money. He did it with the motorcycles but I don't think that it was quite as big with cars. On Bank Holiday Easter Monday, our people preferred to go to Goodwood because that was the elite circuit in those days.

'We used to have six or seven motorcycle meetings and John Surtees was certainly a developing talent in that period. John hit the scene suddenly. He was a contemporary of Bob McIntyre, who had been the top rider. It was obvious that Surtees had the skill. There was something special about him – as was proved in time. John was very focused and determined. Bob McIntyre was also a determined rider and we were friendly with him. Bob was a great favourite of everyone. Alistair King was a great friend but rival of Bob. There were a lot of good riders around at the time with guts and spirit. You needed that to go around Mallory at that sort of speed.

'In the cars, Tommy Dickson of Scotland was a great friend, plus Innes Ireland who used to come to Mallory regularly. He came with a crowd and they stayed overnight – sometimes in the caravans. Tim Parnell was another outstanding driver and raced in Formula One. Bob Gerard did race here – having launched the track. Jim Clark, of course, raced at Mallory in the late 1950s and early 1960s and Graham Hill came along not long afterwards.'

The edition of Autosport of 15 June 1962 covers the most star-studded four-wheel race of the Wormleighton era. For on the front grid were a quartet of those who were amongst the greatest drivers in the history of the sport – in qualifying order they were: Jim Clark (Lotus V8) 51 seconds; Jack Brabham (Lotus V8) 51.6 seconds; Graham Hill (Lotus 4) 52 seconds and John Surtees (Lola V8) 52.6 seconds. The report reads: 'The crowd's appetite was thoroughly whetted

John Surtees receives the Race of the Year trophy from Clive Wormleighton, 1958.

Sir Jack Brabham (right) with John Surtees (centre) no doubt recalling the track action of some forty years previous. Chris Meek is to the left.

when the Formula One cars lined up for the seventy-five-lap race, with a top prize of 2,000 guineas – a fair amount of ackers for a matter of 100 miles. The Nottingham SCC and Mallory Park's Clive Wormleighton certainly dangled a golden bait to bring Grand Prix-style racing to the grand little Leicestershire circuit. When the flag fell Surtees made a superb start and out-accelerated the rest, with Jack Brabham tucking in behind the Lola as Masten Gregory (Lotus) shot ahead of Graham Hill and Jim Clark. Hill took Gregory for third place on lap two while Jo Bonnier (Porsche) moved up in front of T. Shelley (Lotus) and Mike Parkes (Cooper-C). The unfortunate J. Dalton (Lotus) came to rest at the hairpin with petrol starvation and remained there for some time before restarting.

'Surtees soon settled down, breaking the lap record no less than three times in four laps and after five laps led Brabham by four seconds. He took a different line from anyone else on the down-swoop from the hairpin to the pits, hugging the bank close as if on two wheels and holding the Lola almost in the centre of the road as he came out of the left-hander.

'Clark, in the monocoque Lotus, closed up on Graham Hill after shooting past Gregory in the UDT-Laystall Lotus. First pits call was Ian Burgess, who stopped to cure a misfire with the Bryden Brown Cooper. J. Rhodes(Cooper-F) managed to get in front of Shelley's black Lotus and C. Davis (Lotus) kept a few yards ahead of de Beaufort (Porsche).

'Jack Brabham was really pressing on, but Surtees was in dazzling form, holding his four-second advantage with a thumbs up to Reg Parnell every time that he rocketed past the pits. Graham Hill was finding the Walker Lotus a very different car from his BRM and was having to do more correcting than usual. Jim Clark's V8 didn't appear to have its full quota of horse, and he could make little or no impression on Hill. With twenty laps coming up, Mike Parkes was attacking Masten Gregory for fourth place in the ex-Surtees Cooper-Climax, which, at the weigh-in, was something like seventy pounds lighter than Hill's Lotus.

'Into the pits came Clark to complain of low oil pressure, restarting in seventh position behind Bonnier's red Porsche. Parkes swept in front of Gregory, showing what an asset he would be to any Formula One team, as the American was certainly not hanging about.

'By twenty-five laps only half-a-dozen cars were on the same lap, Clark, Rhodes, Davis, de Beaufort, Shelly, Burgess and Dalton all having been doubled by the flying Surtees and the pursuing Brabham. Into the pits came Clark, with no oil pressure at all. An attempt was made to find some by bunging up the breather and the Scotsman eventually re-entered the race many, many laps in arrears.

'The race pattern was set with John Surtees holding off Brabham, Hill safely in third place, and Parkes gradually getting away from Gregory. The last-named was doubled on lap thirty-three and two laps later Parkes waved Surtees past, leaving only the three leaders on the same lap. Rhodes was in trouble, his engine spitting and banging on acceleration. He finally retired on the forty-eighth lap and Clark also gave up the struggle rather than risk a valuable V8 engine needed for Spa the next Sunday.

'Shelley managed to overtake de Beaufort, but otherwise there was no change in the race order. A few laps from the end Brabham made another desperate bid to get to grips with Surtees, but the closest he got was 4.5 seconds. Then he eased off during the final three laps, doubtless with Spa in mind and quite content to hold his second place and collect £500.

'Surtees took the chequered flag 18.2 seconds in front of Brabham and 28.2 seconds in front of Graham Hill, who had put up a magnificent show with the four-cylinder car.

'Leonard Lee presented Surtees with his cheque, which was quickly nicked by assistant race manager Gill Harris. The winner also received a splendid Coventry Cathedral commemoration silver salver from Mrs Leonard Lee, wife of the Coventry Climax chief. Graham Hill, accepting a cheque for £200 commented, 'Hey, isn't there a nought missing?'

John Surtees, winner, F1 race 1962.

The clubhouse at Mallory Park.

Time would soon be called on the Wormleighton era as Cynthia explains: 'By 1962 running Mallory Park had got very demanding. It was a fault of Clive's – he wouldn't delegate. He would delegate to me, of course, but when it came to other people, such as the clubs, Clive wanted to be in control. Looking back at my own role – well we had created the clubhouse. It took a bit of effort to get things going. We had inherited the caterers that the grass-track people used. It was then that we brought in some people from Nuneaton who made a very good job of the outside catering.

'We felt that we needed a focal point and that was what we built – a clubhouse. Then we had to have a members' club, which was organised and mainly involved local people. I started working there and overseeing matters. Generally speaking, from early afternoon I was out dealing with the money. We had a car park firm within time. Originally we had the local fishing club looking after the car park. That didn't prove too satisfactory when the meetings were so popular. So we engaged a company from up North. They did that and took the money. After the meeting I would go to the clubhouse and all the riders or drivers were there too with the staff. They would have a drink or a coffee before setting off. I had a busy day. Clive was out on the circuit and I was busy in the background.

'It got so much, then Reg Parnell said to Clive that if ever he thought of selling, Reg knew somebody who was interested. That was it and it was done. Clive had gone through six hard years. In July he sold the circuit to Grovewood, who owned Brands Hatch. He stayed on to see the diary through but he wouldn't want a situation where other people were telling him what to do. He was a contact point for the clubs as the new owners took over. Come 30 September 1962 that was it. Over the years I am sure he regretted the decision as Mallory Park had been such an important part of his life.

'Once we left Mallory Park we still visited and kept our contacts, particularly with the Overends. Again it was a family-orientated management, as we had been.

'Clive died in 1990 and he would have been proud and delighted to see how the circuit has survived and developed until the present day. I see the fiftieth anniversary as a reflection on Clive as the key player in the circuit's history. I am delighted with the occasion.'

THE GOLDEN YEARS

In July 1962 the *Hinckley Times* published a major story: 'Mallory Park Sold. Mallory Park motor racing circuit has been sold for a figure in excess of £100,000 (believed to be a quarter of a million) to Grovewood Securities Limited, the London property and investment company, which last year acquired Brands Hatch motor racing circuit in Kent. Motor sport will continue as arranged for this season, while next year both competitors and spectators may benefit from intended improvements.

"'We are not afraid to spend money in improving the facilities and making Mallory Park the Brands Hatch of the Midlands. We want to really liven things up as far as motor sport is concerned," said Grovewood's chairman, Mr John Danny.'

The management team at Mallory was to consist of motorcycle director Chris Lowe and group MD John Webb, who offers this insight into events up to and beyond the acquisition: 'In 1961 when I handled PR for Brands Hatch I "found" Grovewood and negotiated their takeover. First year Brands results were good and Grovewood, who had made me a Brands director, asked me to look out for other circuits. Mallory Park was then owned by Clive Wormleighton, with whom I had a mutual friend in ex-Grand Prix driver Reg Parnell of Derby. He told me that Wormleighton wished to sell and resultantly negotiated the purchase for £150,000 in the summer of 1962. Later we bought Snetterton in 1963 and Oulton Park in 1964 to put us in the position of running over fifty per cent of UK car and motorcycle championships and therefore give us a power base to create formulae and championships. Our direction of Mallory was greatly aided by the use of helicopters and aircraft, which landed on the straight, and which brought Mallory to only forty minutes' travel time out of our base at Brands.

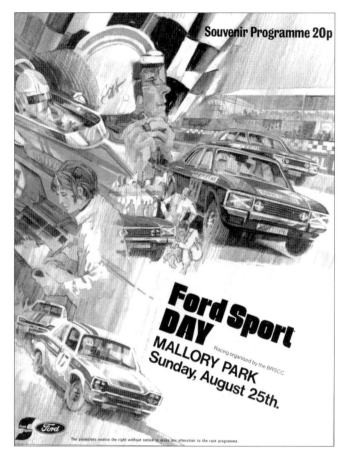

Left: Programme cover, Ford Sport Day.

Opposite: General entertainments.

'Mallory already had the Race of the Year at the time of the takeover but we added the Transatlantic motorcycle series, Sidecar Race of the Year, Ford Sport Days with Grand Prix drivers, Formula 5000, and a momentous Bay City Rollers Day in 1976. We tried powerboat racing on the lake but it neither made nor lost money.'

The development of the Formula Ford concept was very successful and it came about as follows. It was the last Sunday in December 1966. John Webb, as MD of Motor Circuit Developments, the controlling company at Mallory Park, and the late Geoffrey Clarke, the owner of the Motor Racing School organisation at Brands Hatch, were setting up their stands for the 1967 Racing Car Show and met afterwards for a coffee at the Royal Garden Hotel. Clarke explained that engineer/instructor John Thomlinson had modified a school Formula Junior to take standard road tyres and a BMC engine to reduce costs. Clarke said his ambition was to run school races, for the cost of the cars was the main deterrent. It was John Webb's opinion that unknown cars were not

attractive to pupils. The cars had to be seen to also race in public and to have a prestigious name but needed to be under £1,000. John Webb suggested Formula Ford. Ford agreed and offered fifty low-price engines. Henry Taylor was involved as the Ford competition's manager.

John and Geoffrey first approached Bruce McLaren to construct but he turned it down to build Formula Bs for the US market. So they consolidated with Colin Chapman of Lotus, whose statue is now at Mallory Park, and ordered twenty-five converted Juniors as Lotus 51s. The pair obtained RAC approval for the Formula and the Championship. The initial Formula Ford price was £975 per car.

As promised at the launch, major improvements were carried out in the first two years, including spectator stands opposite the start line and at the entrance to Gerard's bend. New commentator, press and timekeepers' boxes were added. Through the 'Golden Years' of the 1960s and 1970s, vast crowds watched both car and motorcycle races that included many international stars. The Post-TT and

Above left: Powerboat racing.

Above right: Colin Chapman's statue.

the Race of the Year continued, with the Transatlantic Match Races also added to the major programme of annual events. With major sponsors for motorcycles – such as the *Daily Mail*, *Daily Express* and Carreras, together with Shell, BP, Guards, John Player and Yellow Pages for cars – and large prize funds on offer, Mallory prospered.

During Whit weekend 1964 a three-hour saloon car race was held. This, a qualifying event for the European Touring Car championship, contributed to a crowded programme also including F2 and F3 racing. Only just arriving back at the circuit in time, so as not to disappoint the large crowd of some 30,000, was Jim Clark, straight from the Indy 500 practice. Jim drove his Lotus 30 and 32 to win both the Guards Trophy Sports Car Race and the thirty-lap Grovewood Trophy F2 race. Another young Scottish driver excelled himself on the day. Twenty-four-year-old Jackie Stewart, driving for the first time ever at Mallory Park, won both the F3 and GT races, setting up a new lap record in the GT race. Now Sir Jackie Stewart, a three times World Formula One Champion and subsequent team constructor, he says of that day: 'I recall my Whitsun victories at Mallory Park in 1964 clearly. I won both the F3 and GT races but the latter

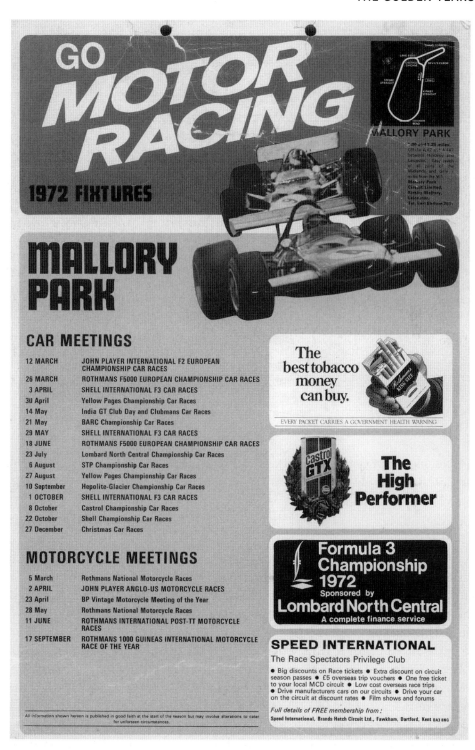

A 1972 fixtures poster.

Sir Jackie Stewart.

was an important victory. Having won a few F3 races, the impact of the GT race was greater as I was in the early days of my race career. I beat the established drivers Peter Arundel and Mike Spence, who competed in factory Elans. I drove the 'Chequered Flag' Elan. This performance was a stepping-stone to winning the British Championship.

'In the F3 race that day I was on pole position and led from start to finish in a comparatively uneventful race. Although I again led from start to finish in the GT race, it was very competitive and I was under constant pressure from the leading lights, including Trevor Taylor. It was my first year of racing and that day at Mallory Park could be regarded as my breakthrough.

'Incidentally, I was a fan of Bob Gerard and have his autograph. He raced ERAS and I saw him at various circuits competing against my brother, Jimmy Stewart. Bob was retiring about the time I went racing so I can't recall racing against him. The bend named after him is most distinctive. On a relatively short track, as Mallory is, time could be gained there if you got your entry to the exit right. On the Mallory track distance, get Gerard's wrong and you would find he recovery period costly. So you had to get it right.

'In later years – during the early 1970s when I was at Tyrrell – I recall attending a Ford Festival and driving a Matra. They had Escorts and Capris on track that day. To me, Mallory always seemed a circuit for enthusiasts. They were different to crowds at other tracks and the trip up there was always a good day out. In those days you would take part in lots of races and I also enjoyed watching from the infield at Mallory. It was not only the spectators who had an excellent view of the drivers!

'Of course, while the racing scene was very convivial, it was also a lot more dangerous when you look back on it. Not just at Mallory but across Europe and America too. Not only for drivers but marshals and spectators too. It only dawned on me as my career progressed that safety at circuits was inadequate. At Gerard's there was no deceleration area but a grass bank on one side, which you could go over the top of, and a lake on the inner line. If a driver had an accident there in my day he was in trouble. The Mallory hairpin came up at a high speed and had slabs alongside and a tree. Once you had negotiated that the Devil's Elbow had to be looked out for and that was tricky too. So the track was challenging. Still, I had some great scraps there!'

It was in June 1966 that Denny Hulme set a lap record of 47.6 seconds (102.10mph) during the Grovewood Trophy for Group 7 two-seater sports cars, thereby smashing the elusive Mallory 100mph lap and Graham Hill and Frank Gardner's previous lap record of 51.8 seconds (93.82mph) set the previous year. He went home £100 richer! Another milestone in Mallory's car racing history was during June 1968 when Roy Pike in his Titan F3 achieved the first 100mph lap for these cars.

Following the big 1960s racing, at the end of that decade Formula 5000 arrived, followed later by the Aurora Formula One Championship. Upon their arrival lap records began to drop dramatically as these powerful cars raced around the tight circuit. Finally, in 1979 Ricardo Zurino in his Arrows A18 Cosworth established a fastest lap of 40.065 seconds, some 121.32mph.

Midweek testing has always formed a large part of Mallory's activities and during the late 1980s and early 1990s both Keke Rosberg (Williams F1) and Nelson Piquet (Brabham F1) established unofficial lap times of well under 40 seconds, Rosberg being clocked at 36 seconds! Jonathan Palmer (Porsche) and Julian Bailey (Nissan) have also been timed at under 40 seconds. The first Formula Ford 1600 100mph lap was established by Vincenzo Sospiri (Van Diemen RF88) of 48.44 seconds, 100.41 mph in 1988.

Mallory has obviously been the scene of many memorable car races and over the years has hosted great names and events, the European F2 Championship, Aurora F1, Shell 5000 and British Touring Cars to name but a few. However, the majority verdict on the greatest car race at Mallory Park is one won by former World Champion motorcyclist and future Formula One World Champion John Surtees.

Ricardo Zurino.

A rare Alpine A360 F3 powered by a Renault-based 16 engine, F3 support race, 1972.

Programme cover, Euro 5000 Championship 1973.

AURORA® AFX
Formula 1

MALLORY PARK

THE Sun

FORMULA 1 TROPHY

(A Qualifying Round of the 1979 Aurora-AFX British Formula 1 Championship)

BANK HOLIDAY MONDAY 7 MAY

Qualifying: Sunday 6 May

Official
Programme 50p

Above: F2 International 1971.

Opposite: Programme cover, Aurora F1 1977.

Formula 2, 1971.

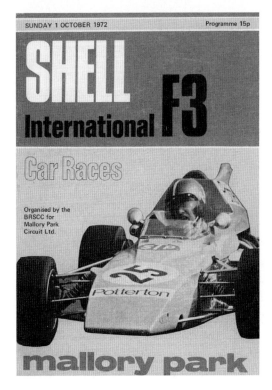

Shell International F3, 1972.

Above left: Rally Cross, 1978.　　　　*Above right:* Super Ford 2000, 1978.

The race run in May 1967 was held in terrible conditions and, to quote *Autosport*: 'John Surtees, using a Cosworth Ford engine in his Lola T100, once again demonstrated his tremendous skill in difficult conditions by running away with last Sunday's abominably wet Guards trophy Formula Two International.' With two ten-lap heats and a seventy-five-lap final Surtees won by three laps. A heroic drive by Jackie Ickx in his Tyrrell Matra pushed Surtees nearly all the way but a big spin around Gerard's lost him second place to Frank Gardner (Brabham BT23), with Bruce McLaren (McLaren 4A) third. In the Saturday dry practice both Jackie Ickx and Alan Rees set fastest times of 46.6 seconds (104.29mph), beating the record of Denny Hulme in his Lola T70, although this was not an official record as it was not made in an actual race.

As for motorcycling, the 1971 Race of the Year is the one everyone still talks about and is probably the greatest race ever at Mallory Park. This race took place on 19 September and John Cooper and Giacomo Agostini battled it out, with the lead changing many times with Cooper on his privately entered 750 BSA taking the flag over the World Champion on his MV Agusta 500. Being a local lad, the huge crowd roared Cooper on and their cheering even drowned out the noise of the bikes. John Cooper indeed had a long and happy association with Mallory Park as he recalls: 'In 1952, when I was a lad, a fellow across the road

Above: Jackie Ickx.

Left: John Cooper.

from me asked me if I would like to go and see some motorbike grass-track racing at Mallory Park. Of course it was then a complete oval. They used to go anti-clockwise for the solos and clockwise for the sidecars. I remember Bill Boddice riding there and he became a champion on the road circuits. People used to ride grass-track and road racing, trials, and scrambles, unlike now, where they specialise in one thing or another.

'I first went there in 1956 when it became a road-race circuit. I remember Percy Tait on a Beasley Velocette. I thought that he was quite old – but he was probably about twenty-four because he isn't that much older than me in reality! Once I started racing I went to ride at Mallory Park and I hadn't got much money. So Clive Wormleighton let me stay in the clubhouse the night before. He was the first man who ever paid me anything. A tremendous man really.

'I can remember winning my first of three Race of the Year titles in 1965. Mike Hailwood, Phil Read and Bill Ivy were the big guys with the works machinery. I was a young lad with a 500 Norton. It sprinkled with rain just before the race and those fast bikes weren't very easy to ride in the wet. I pinched the 1,000 guineas prize, which was a lot of money in those days. Most people were earning £20 a week. I won it again on my Yamsel 350 in 1970. It rained a bit that day. Then came 1971 and the race against Agostini.

'I rode for the BSA team because they had a spare bike and they wanted another member to ride for Britain against America in match races at Brands, Mallory and Oulton. I was one of the top scorers at all three meetings. I had

Mike Hailwood.

Phil Read.

this factory BSA Triple. They had Percy Tait, Tony Jefferies and Ray Pickerell. I rode the spare bike. It was a lovely bike and I've never ridden one that I liked better than that. After the match races it went back to the factory, just as a spare bike. Then I said to the BSA factory, "Look here. Is there any chance of buying that bike for the Race of the Year?" They replied that they were too committed and didn't have the mechanics or anything to work on the bike. I stated, "If you let me ride that bike in the Race of the Year I will win it. I'll beat anybody, it's such a good bike." They kept telling me that it was impossible to lend it to me. So I went to see Peter Deverell who was the MD there and I reiterated, "Look Peter, if you'll let me ride that bike in the Race of the Year I am sure that I can win it." He said that he would take me down to see Doug Hele and told Doug, "This lad has got to race at Mallory Park in the Race of the Year on the BSA that he rode in the match races." Doug commented that it was only a standard engine – it was only a hack bike. He emphasised, "So I will tell you what we will do. You can take it to Mallory and you can test it." So we went to Mallory Park for tests. Every lap I broke the lap record and they couldn't believe it. They thought that I must be taking a short cut. Anyway they kept gearing the bike up and the rest is history.

'I went to Mallory Park. All the riders wanted it to be an engine-running start because lots had 750 twins, which were difficult to push-start. Giacomo Agostini pointed out that it was in the regulations that it should be a push-start. So a push-start it was. Anyway, I had to run a long way to land on the seat – it went – and I just beat Agostini. He led me and I led him. I can remember passing him on the tenth lap out of thirty laps. I could hear the crowd cheer. It was unbelievable. I didn't think it was possible you could hear plus take in all their waving and carrying on! The place was packed, however. Agostini had received £2,000 as starting money and I got £100! Anyway I ended up with a thousand guineas and I won the 500 race as well. So the outsider came home from Mallory that day with close on £2,000 in his pocket.'

Motor Cycle News' reporting team of Norrie Whyte and John Brown were covering the event. *MCN*'s report in the following Wednesday's edition is reprinted here… many will still be saying: 'I was there!'

'Fifty thousand sun-drenched fans at Sunday's Race of the Year cheered John Cooper's finest half-hour. On a works three-cylinder BSA, he scored his second successive £1,050 win in Mallory Park's international Race of the Year by beating Giacomo Agostini and the MV-3 fair and square.

'After thirty laps of the 1.35-mile Leicestershire circuit, each packed with tension and drama, Cooper won by three-fifths of a second from Ago.

'After congratulating Cooper, Ago said, "It was a hot race. Cooper is a fine rider. I was having to turn off the power halfway round Gerard's and this was where I was losing ground. I had too much power."

'As starter Mr George Padley released fifty-seven cylinders and twenty-six machines at the second attempt from the Race of the Year's first clutch start, Ago and Cooper stormed into the lead and the whole pack surged past Phil Read, on the front row with Cooper's Yamsel as his own Yamahas were out of action.

'In third place behind Agostini and Cooper for four laps and splitting the Triumph-BSA team with Percy Tait, Ray Pickrell and Paul Smart on his tail, Barry Sheene crashed the 500 Suzuki twin at Gerard's on lap five. He escaped with severe bruising and hopes to clinch the 125cc World Championship in Spain on Sunday.

'This left the British Superbikes and Ago's MV in the first five places after five laps. And that's the way it stayed, for none of the 350 Yamahas was fast enough to live with the pace of the bigger bikes.

'Jarno Saarinen, riding his 250 Yamaha as his 350 was handling badly, was battling with Tony Rutter for sixth place, ahead of Mike Hailwood, who had passed Derek Chatterton and Steve Machin.

Agostini leads Cooper with Sheene in pursuit, 1971.

'To a great cheer from the crowd, Cooper got the better of Agostini at Gerard's on lap ten to take a lead that he held for five laps. In that time Cooper survived a heart-stopping lock-to-lock skid at the Esses on lap fourteen when he just managed to keep ahead of Ago. Next lap, slightly detuned, Cooper took it steady there and Ago shot past.

'Behind the leaders Pickrell and Smart got ahead of Tait as the pace speeded up. Hailwood retired when a piston pin broke, Rutter stopped with a seized Yam, and Read, beginning to get the hang of the Yamsel, pulled through the field.

'By distances varying from thirty yards to a couple of inches, Ago led until the twenty-second lap. Then Coop dived inside Ago at the Esses. And that was the crucial move, for it was the last time the lead changed.

'Ago tried everything he knew, skirting the guardrail at the exit of Devil's Elbow by a fraction of an inch. So did Cooper. Times were consistently near the lap record of 52 seconds, but the Cooper-Hailwood record wasn't broken, possibly because of oil on the hairpin, which needed great care and a wider line than usual. By the end of the forty-one miles, Cooper won by a fraction of a second. He and Ago were 17 seconds ahead of Pickrell, who held off his constant shadow, Smart.

'After retiring, Hailwood watched the rest of the race. He said, "Best race I've ever seen. Really puts the riders into perspective doesn't it?"'

John Cooper would seem to agree: 'It is a race that will go down in history. Yes, it was a great race and as a result of winning the Race of the Year I was invited to America to compete in the Ontario Classic, which was in California. They shipped me out with the mechanics and the bike. There I did win the Ontario Classic and $15,000. It was over 100 degrees. 125 miles, a forty-five-minute break during which you could change tyres, and another 125 miles. I actually beat Kel Carruthers by four inches! On the last lap Kel had got quite a way in front of me. I had to race really, really hard and came off the banking at 160mph, sliding and shaking. As we went past Kel's wife, he was in front of me by about a bike's length. However, I crossed the line first. When we got to the big circle for the winner, they put me in it. Jacky Carruthers ran up and exclaimed, "You pommie bastard!" because he received $6,000 and I got $15,000. Quite a difference!

'So the Mallory success gave me that break. People who were there in 1971 still talk about it today. I've got a motorbike shop in Derby and folk still come in and tell me that they were there. I thought everybody was dead who was there then! There still seem a lot of people around who were there in their twenties. At that time I was thirty-four years old, so I suppose the memories will last for a few more years yet.

'Agostini wasn't very pleased because he was riding the works MV. He wasn't supposed to go anywhere unless he could beat everyone. They didn't like being beaten. Anyway, when I went to Brands the next weekend, I stayed in the same hotel as Giacomo. He said to me, "I've got a works engine this week. Last week we only had the practice engine." I replied, "It's a funny thing, Giacomo, but they've upgraded mine as well!" I then went out and beat him at Brands as well. I then beat him at Cadwell Park but people don't seem to remember those facts.

'Afterwards you are so tired. It's a big thing and you don't really realise what an achievement it was. The British fans loved it. There can't be many riders who have heard a big cheer when you pass somebody going into the Esses at Mallory or anywhere else for that matter. When I won everybody went absolutely wild. They loved it.

'I can also remember in 1971 before the Race of the Year when the 500 race was on. As I said, I rode in the 500 race as well. Barry Sheene was in it. He had a bit of a dice with Agostini and so I pointed out to him, "When you fire in the Race of the Year, Barry, your times are not going to match Ago's and mine. Just be careful because I know that you are not going to beat us but third place is for the taking." Barry was a cocky Cockney. I helped him when he first started and he used to come and stop with me. We were good friends. Well, I looked around at the hairpin on the second lap and Barry was a few yards behind me. I came around on the fourth lap and there were caution flags. I looked around and there is Barry laying in a hedge bottom. I thought, "Oh dear!" When I eventually got back to the pits I shouted, "I bloody well told you Barry – be careful – finish third. You knew that it was there for you." He replied, "My footrest caught the ground." I said, "Yes, they do when you fall off!" I've had lots of really good races at Mallory – it has been really good as a home base.'

What of the Mallory memories of John's great rival – the legendary multi-World Champion Giacomo Agostini? 'I won my first set of races at Mallory Park and these were in the 350, 500 and 1,000 classes. Although Mallory Park was a short circuit, it was also very difficult. Gerard's was a very long curve and very demanding to hold your position on. I raced in a very competitive era and went to Mallory Park after the TT races to face such as Mike Hailwood, Phil Read and John Cooper. There was a lot of British motorcycling talent.

'The hairpin had its obvious demands too. You could lose at least half a second there, which could be over 10 seconds in a race. You had to keep on the pace, keep the revs up and go faster coming out.

'I only raced a small number of meetings per year on the British tracks and didn't have the opportunity for extensive prior practice. So you had the added challenge of track specialists. John Cooper was the serious rival at Mallory Park while Derek Minter was the man to watch at Brands Hatch. Power range was a factor in those close races, plus handling the gears at a place like Mallory was crucial too.

'Besides John Cooper, I had some great races with Mike Hailwood – particularly in the Grand Prix – here, there and everywhere. But taking Mike on at Mallory, as I said, added to the challenge.

'I can remember that my racing schedule at Mallory was very demanding. I would be on track at 9 a.m. and, if successful, be still racing at 5 p.m. I mentioned that I took part in the 350, 500 and 1,000cc classes and there would be heats before finals, of course. All those lovely girls lined up who wanted to meet me and I was too tired to do anything about it!

'I raced at the Post-TT in June and the Race of the Year in September. I enjoyed victories at Mallory Park in all or most finals consecutively from 1966 to 1971 with further successes in the mid-1970s.

'Ago' receives a winners' cheque at Mallory Park.

'Of course I remember that race with John Cooper at the Race of the Year in 1971. It was very close and his machine was on 100 per cent performance. I kept losing to him at the hairpin and I lost him one time too many. He beat me when I was on the works Agusta and I respect him for that. I know that he will tell you more details of that race in the book – he's keener to talk about it!

'I have kept my links with Mallory Park over the years and was always friendly with the Overend family, who did such a great job when they took over in 1983. I hope that the new management can keep Mallory as 'The Friendly Circuit' – a title that it richly deserves. I am told that the new man in charge – John Ward – is a knowledgeable motor sport enthusiast with lots of circuit experience. That is good news. I have been back for an exhibition at Mallory Park and have taken a lap of honour. I look forward to returning soon to a circuit that I shall always have fond memories of.'

One of the other great races on the circuit took place at the 1987 Race of the Year when Roger Marshall and Fred Merkel battled it out in pouring rain. Although Merkel fell off at Gerard's on the last lap, the race winner's award was given to him. However, following Marshall's vigorous protests the original decision was overturned and Marshall declared the winner. Fred Merkel had

Happy times for 'Ago'.

'Ago' and John Cooper relive memories in 1999.

Roger Marshall receives his trophy from Edwina Overend.

rushed off back to the States with the winner's trophy, so a new trophy had to be made. It was finally presented to Roger Marshall at the next EMRA dinner.

In 1971 Chris Lowe, the motor circuit development bike director, inaugurated a new series – the Anglo-American match races appropriately called the Transatlantic races. An Easter fixture from 1971 to 1986, the surprising issue isn't that the event lasted so long but the fact that they started at all. In 1971 the American Motorcyclist Association (AMA) had only just ended over half a century's isolation from world motorcycle sport. The country whose top riders had come home 1–2–3 on Indian twins in the first senior TT on the Isle of Man in 1911 had developed styles of competition in isolation. From 1954, the AMA demanded that national champions be more expert on loose dirt and shale than tarmac. Road racing came way down the list of desirable skills. Those US riders who did venture across the ocean to Britain and Europe soon discovered that they had a lot of ground to make up. However, that was the biggest surprise of the early Transatlantic match races – the Americans were quick learners!

'Riding in England taught us a lot. I think it made us better racers,' says Dave Aldana, a veteran of cold Easter rides. 'I'd never raced in rain before, but I realised that the technique was simple. If you didn't throttle back, you were an idiot and you deserved to fall down.'

Dick Mann had few illusions about the US team's chances in 1971. 'I took it for granted that we'd get beaten,' he says. 'But in fact I was surprised at how close we were to the lap records. You must remember that some members of the team had hardly done any road racing.'

What enabled the series – with races at Brands Hatch, Mallory Park and Oulton Park – to get off the ground was BSA-Triumph's vision. By providing three-cylinder 750 Triumph Trident and BSA Rocket 3 racers for all team members they gave the first event an air of equal competition. It was also a brilliant marketing exercise for models that were aimed at the world's richest market for motorcycles – North America. A back-up squad of 650 Bonneville twins was held in reserve. So the US team, led by Gary Nixon, comprised Dick Mann, Dave Aldana, Don Castro, Jim Rice and Don Emde. Britain's captain Percy Tait was supported by a solid array of experienced road racing talent – John Cooper, Ray Pickrell, Paul Smart and Tony Jefferies.

The problem with organising international road racing events in England at Easter centres on the fact that this religious festival moves from year to year by almost as much as a month. Early spring weather in Kent, Leicestershire and Cheshire is completely unpredictable. Look out for rain, hail, snow, fog or brilliant sunshine! The opening round in 1971 at Brands Hatch was cold and miserable. Ray Pickrell was the star, winning both races, but both Dick Mann and Don Castro performed well.

Mallory Park presented the US team with a steeper leaning curve. Nowhere had they seen a circuit with a first-gear hairpin approached via a series of fast, deceptive S-bends, or a corner like Gerard's, which just seems to go on and on, forever. Master of Mallory John Cooper put on a fine display but couldn't top the flying Pickrell, with many riders falling and Dick Mann proving that he was truly Mr Reliable.

It was Paul Smart's chance to shine at Oulton Park, winning in devastating style. Dick Mann took fourth and second places, while John Cooper bagged a brace of thirds. The series ended with Great Britain winning 183 points to 137, with US top scorer Mann only two points down on Pickrell and Smart's 48 points apiece. More importantly, the series had proved a hit with the riders, public and media. This led to John Player sponsorship – and a change of title to the Transatlantic Trophy – later picked up by Marlboro. Over sixteen years the US won on only four occasions. But that really wasn't the point of the Anglo-American matches. In the early years they saw American riders grasp new skills in an alien environment and climate, ending the isolation in which road racing had become unimportant. British fans gained an insight into their favourite

Right: Ron Haslam – one
of the success stories of the
Transatlantic series.

Below: Paul Smart.

sport by watching talented newcomers grapple with its challenges. Mixing two nations, a common language and widely differing traditions was a brave experiment, but it worked. There were surprise victors and equally surprising losers. But the real winners were those thousands of fans for whom Easter simply meant the Transatlantic.

Paul Smart provides his perspective: 'I absolutely loved the Transatlantic races. I was team captain two or three times. I did miss a couple of years because I left these shores and got a job in America. The collapse of the BSA-Triumph organisation meant that I was out of a job in 1972. I went to work with Kawasaki so I missed one or two years. When I came back after two years there was an argument as to who I should be riding for – America or Britain. That's a nice situation to be in. I was one of the few people who knew a lot of American riders for I had ridden over there. The first series was in 1971. The atmosphere was fabulous. It was right at the beginning of the season and was the whole Easter weekend. Brands on the Friday, travel up for Mallory on the Sunday with Oulton Park on the Monday. A great weekend.

'It was so popular that the hardest part was getting to the circuit in the morning. You had to be very early because the practising was there on the day. Initially it was the BSA-Triumphs, which was one of the most wonderful noises ever.

'It was a hell of a busy day. We would turn up in the morning for 8 a.m. practice so you had to be at the circuit at 6.30 a.m. Otherwise you couldn't get in because the queues were amazing. We used to stay at Hinckley or Leicester. It was a hell of a crack and we loved it.

'The majority of the American team, in fact, had very little road-racing experience. They rode in this category only about half-a-dozen times a year. The lack of strength led to some funny circumstances. On the first Transatlantic series I think it was John Cooper who suggested to some of the team that they went a little bit slower so that the Americans could keep up and make it more interesting. Unfortunately he hadn't been around and spoken to everybody – I wouldn't agree. The slower goers could get excited and actually think that they were catching up. That usually ends in a tangle. That is exactly what happened. There was a pile-up so it didn't do anybody any good. Yes, that was a problem in the first place because we had about three Americans who were very good. Cal Rayborn was the one. The others were Gary Nixon and Dick Mann. Lots of the other guys most people had never heard of. Some had apparently not taken part in road races at all. They were incredibly enthusiastic and they had an unbelievable riding style. Some of these guys put their foot down at the hairpin and stuff like that. They certainly were raw. It's difficult to compare one generation to another but it was almost a generation apart. There was no reverse arrangement. It wouldn't have worked in America as the circuits were so far apart.

Gary Nixon with Edwina Overend.

'Chris Lowe was very much involved. Chris was very much the boss then. He was a fair man and always treated me fairly for a man with control of motorcycle sport, at this level, in this country. The company owned several of the important circuits. I had some idea of what the others riders received. He wasn't going to tell you how much he was paying anybody else. You would negotiate your own start money.

'Chris was the sort of person who, when you got to a certain level, would come and make you an offer. Invariably it wasn't negotiable – he obviously had his sums to do. I do think that riders such as Mike Hailwood, Barry Sheene and Kenny Roberts were in the big league when it came to deals. In my day it was a few hundreds at the most.

'The Transatlantic series was great fun because of the camaraderie really, plus the fact that you were in teams. There was no other road racing where you were in a team, so you had to be friends with a domestic rival. I was captain on several occasions and this was a decision made by the organisers. You didn't really have much to do but you had to be a pretty consistent performer to get chosen. Then you dealt with the media primarily.'

Keith Heuwen had a less conventional introduction to these Transatlantic races: 'I qualified for my first Transatlantic races in 1979. I was among a group

Mike Hailwood.

of young, up-and-coming riders invited to try for one of the three places on offer. You would be judged on performance and the media were assembled in the new Kentagon at Brands Hatch. I had to be hauled out of the pits and taken along. I remember that after my name was announced and I was introduced, Barry Sheene's first ever words to me were: "I've never f——ing heard of you, mate!"

'Obviously I got to know Barry well and he was ahead of his time in so many ways. He understood the whole jigsaw required to compete in the sport. For me the Transatlantic series were fantastic events but had a steep learning curve coming up against riders such as Kenny Roberts Senior. It may have been testing but it was also very convivial. Steve Parrish and Barry Sheene were the jokers in the pack. We all travelled together and stayed together over the weekend.

'Mallory was particularly challenging. Flat out through the Esses and then turning at the hairpin on tyres with a four-inch rim. Also motors were more prone to seize in those days and there wasn't the safety movement of the current era. To be frank, Mallory was a bit basic in many ways. Gerard's still stands out as one of the most technically interesting bends of any circuit I raced. You could get held up for an eternity and have to go under or through opponents. You couldn't just chuck it in there. Standards may have changed. Gerard's hasn't!'

Carlos Reutemann, Peter Westbury, Derek Bell and Niki Lauda, 1971.

For the young Keith it was as if a switch was thrown when he came to Mallory, for he was always at the front of the field. In 1980 at Mallory he was at the top of the British points. The Transatlantic series gave Keith his big chance to go on to an active top-class career. Not that the four-wheel action at Mallory wasn't progressive. In March 1971 Formula Two returned to the venue. For some time F2 had been absent from Grovewood venues. Motor Circuit Developments had decided that the formula was too expensive for them, because it involved graded drivers. Formula 5000 was introduced in its place. March 1972 saw the first ever race for the two-litre Formula Two cars at Mallory. Favourites Niki Lauda, Carlos Reutemann, Jody Scheckter and retiree Ronnie Peterson were all beaten by David Morgan in a Brabham.

Other activities were also introduced such as sailing boats, speedboats, hydroplanes and water skiing. The venue had also been utilised as a rally stage and a stage of the World Cycling Championship. Radio One Fun and Race Days featured prominently in the 1970s. In May 1975 a huge crowd attended, most of whom seemed to want to see the Bay City Rollers. It is reported that by the presence of the pop stars thousands of girls were sent 'into screams of ecstasy and then the first-aid hut', before they 'inevitably ran amok, invading the track and the lake, and holding up racing for an hour'. Obviously this proved tedious for genuine motor racing fans and the problems engendered resulted in such occasions becoming transitory events at Mallory Park!

Birrel (nearest), Descarolo (middle) and Petersen (farthest) lay rubber at the start of the Speed International, March 1971.

Carlos Reutemann.

Ronnie Peterson.

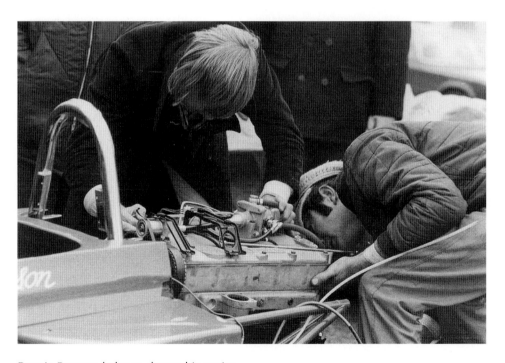

Ronnie Peterson helps to change his engine.

Above: 1972, F2. Ronnie Petersen in the long coat at the rear of the March 722 struggles with a Cosworth BBA engine. A spare engine waits on the stand alongside.

Left: A rear view of Ronnie Petersen's works March 722, showing the installation of Cosworth BDA engine and massive air box. Full 2-litre engines were allowed in 1972.

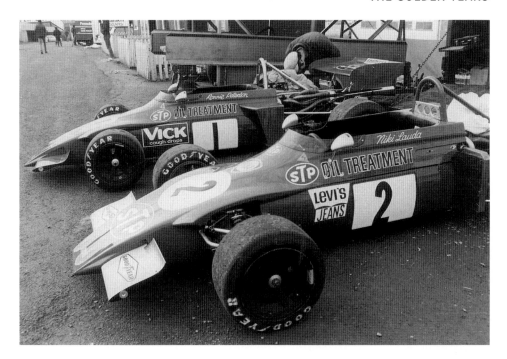

Above: Pair of works March 722s in the paddock. Future F1 World Champion Niki Lauda went on to finish second to Dave Morgan's Brabham BT-36. A little later the 722 chassis formed the basis of the F5000 car, then eventually an F1 car.

Right: John Surtees gets to warm up Mike Hailwood's new Matchbox Surtees TS10 FZ car.

The first F2 Brabham to use a monocoque was works-backed and signalled the new body shapes to emerge from Brabham.

Jean-Pierre Jabouille drove this Elf-Coombs Racing March 722 with Ford-Hart BDA engine. Note the cardboard and tape covering over the side radiator to help the engine warm up quickly on this bitterly cold day.

Jean-Pierre Jabouille.

The mainstay engine in F2 for 1972 was
the Ford RS 1600-based engine, updated
by Cosworth to full 2-litre BDA standard,
as seen awaiting fitting to Petersen's March.

1972 – in the supporting F3 race, Jeremy Gambs entered his Ensign with Vegahtune-Ford engine.

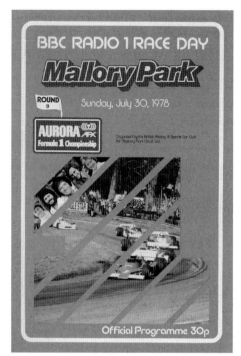

Above left: The Radio One roadshow.

Above right: Radio One roadshow and race day.

James Hunt.

John Player
Race of the Year

RACE 4	Start: 3.00	40 LAPS

by Invitation of Motor Circuit Developments

No.	Rider/Entrant	Town or Country	cc	Machine
1	ROGER MARSHALL/George Beale	Binbrook	750	Yamaha
2	KENNY ROBERTS	USA	750	Yamaha
3	GREGG HANSFORD/Team Kawasaki	Australia	750	Yamaha
4	RON HASLAM/Mal Carter	Langley Mill	750	Pharoah Yamaha
5	JOHN NEWBOLD/J. M. Newbold – Ray Hamblin M/cs	South Normanton	747	Yamaha
6	STEVE PARRISH/Makaha Skateboards – Team Castrol	Royston	750	Yamaha
7	BARRY SHEENE/Texaco Heron Team Suzuki	Charlwood	653	Suzuki
8	DAVE POTTER/Team BP – Broad Motors	Orpington	750	Broad Yamaha
9	ALEX GEORGE	Holland	750	Yamaha
10	MICK GRANT/Team Kawasaki	Lepton	750	Kawasaki
11	STAN WOODS/Swindon Albion Racing	Chester	750	Suzuki
12	BARRY DITCHBURN/Sid Griffiths Racing	West Kingsdown	750	Yamaha
14	STEVE MANSHIP/Wide Range Honda Centre	Leicester	750	Maxton Yamaha
16	DENNIS IRELAND/Derry's Racing	Heston	750	Suzuki
18	TONY RUTTER/R. W. Priest	Brierley Hill	748	Yamaha
19	STEVE WRIGHT/Len Manchester M/cs – Team Castrol	Barnsley	500	Manchester Suzuki
20	KEVIN STOWE/Harold Coppock	Grimsby	750	Coppock Suzuki
23	WIL HARTOG/Texaco Heron Team Suzuki	Holland	852	Suzuki
24	CHARLIE WILLIAMS/Gerald Brown	Warrington	750	Yamaha
27	TOM HERRON	N. Ireland	750	Yamaha
31	JEFF SAYLE	Australia	750	Yamaha
33	BERNARD FAU	France	747	Kawasaki
34	BERNARD MURRAY/D. Johnson & White City M/cs	Stockport	748	White City Maxton
36	PIERRE SOULAS	France	750	Yamaha
40	BOB SMITH/R. D. McCutcheon	St. Helens	750	Yamaha
50	CHRISTIAN SARRON/Sonauto Gauloises G.P.A.	France	750	Yamaha
51	PATRICK PONS/Sonauto Gauloises G.P.A.	France	750	Yamaha
69	JEAN-CLAUDE MEILLAND	France	354	Yamaha
89	HUBERT RIGAL/Moto-club de Monaco	Monaco	747	Yamaha

Reserves (in order of fastest practice times)

54	VIC SOUSAN/George Beale	France	347	Yamaha
68	EERO HYVARINEN	Finland	347	Yamaha
28	JOHN COWIE/Premier Motors	Worchester Park	347	Yamaha
91	PHIL MELLOR	Shelley	500	Suzuki
75	MARC FONTAN	France	348	Yamaha
22	DEREK CHATTERTON/Chatterton Motors	Boston	748	Chat Yamaha
66	INGO REIMER	West Germany	748	Yamaha

RECORDS

1	S. Baker		48.0 101.25 11.9.76
40			

RESULTS

1st (£1500)	7	2nd (£750)	23	3rd (£400)	2	4th (£250)	1	5th (£100)	51
6th (£75)	12	7th (£50)	5	8th (£25)	6	9th (£15)	18	10th (£10)	89
11th	33	12th	24	13th		14th		15th	

Winner's Time ___33 Min___ Speed ___98·18___ mph
Fastest Lap: No. ___7/23___ Time ___48·7 Sec___ Speed ___99·79___ mph

The Race of the Year, 1977.

A distinctive occasion of a different nature had taken place in 1973 when Lord Hesketh and his Hesketh Racing Team, with driver James Hunt, arrived at Mallory Park to contest the Formula Two series. The team workers, in matching outfits of T-shirts, jackets and trousers, set up the new Surtees TS15 while 'a steady procession of helicopters and limousines ferried in Lord Hesketh's entourage with their needs attended to by a liveried butler who dispensed champagne and caviar'. The Hesketh party proceeded to enjoy themselves boisterously as if they were at some kind of country house weekend. Such antics received a mixed reception from observers, but the team was very serious and professional. However, on this occasion, off-track activities were not matched by success on the track, with James Hunt's retirement following the shedding of his car's front wheel. Within three years he did become Formula One World Champion, of course.

By the mid-1970s over thirty meetings a year were being held at the circuit. Two-thirds at that time were for cars, the remainder for motorcycles. In August 1977 a round of the British Fusegear Formula Ford Championship was won by the 'promising Birmingham driver' Nigel Mansell in a Crossle 32F. A fortnight later, the same driver proved unbeatable in the Townsend Thoresen Formula Ford 1600 Championship race. In fact, Nigel had won his first race at Mallory Park. This was in 1976 driving a Formula Ford. As the great British racer and Formula One World Champion recalls: 'What I know about my first career victory in 1976 at Mallory was that it was in the wet and I remember driving around Gerard's corner overtaking people on the outside – it was a great race. As for my performance in August 1977, the British Fusegear Championship final was at Silverstone but winning the race at Mallory did set me up for the championship that year. The later victory at Mallory that season helped me realise my potential at this point. I feel that every race you win in whatever formula secures great confidence for any driver and obviously in my case I went on from strength to strength.

'The circuit will always hold fond memories for me as it was great to watch other races when you were working on the car in the middle of the circuit and then, standing on the back of the trailer, I was able to watch the other categories and just the whole environment was friendly at Mallory Park.

'My general impression was of sport at its grass-roots level when the majority of people helped one another and embraced the sport for what it was. There was noise, excitement and enthusiasm and you always felt part of it at Mallory Park, possibly because it was a small circuit and you were always aware of things going on around you. It is great to have this opportunity now to thank all the people who were involved with Mallory Park during my formative years.'

Nigel, of course, was very familiar with Don Truman as a clerk of the course at Mallory. Don, along with the much younger Bruce Widdowson of the Nottingham Sports Car Club, had hands-on experience of all the eras of

Mallory's history under consideration. For now, here are their memories of the original Wormleighton and subsequent Webb management of the circuit, starting with octogenarian Don: 'I took up driving in 1947. I won the first race held at Oulton Park in a 500 in 1953. Lots of circuits opened in the early 1950s. I was living in Walsall at the time that Mallory came along in 1956. This was good news as it wasn't far away. The first car meeting was a closed-to-club occasion and I was in the next one. I raced regularly there after that and so saw the early history and development of Mallory Park. Mallory was just right for the 500s but seeing them drive the 5000s around was frightening! I finished racing at the last Silverstone meeting of 1959. The following week I went to Oulton Park as a marshal. John Henderson was then clerk of the course and always ran Mallory too. I got to Oulton Park at 8 a.m. It chucked it down all day like stair rods. I finished at eight at night. That was the start.

'At Mallory I took on the role of observer for the Nottingham Car Club in 1960. I did two or three meetings. In the late 1950s I had got involved with the BRSCC and by 1961 was on the committee. That year we had a meeting at my house in Walsall. We had been asked to race at Mallory Park. I remember saying, "That's fair enough. Who is going to be clerk of the course?" They said, "You are!"

1956.

1957.

1957.

1958.

1958.

1959.

1959.

I didn't have to go on a modular course as they have to these days. I was an ex-driver and knew what it was all about. Then – if the club said that you were a clerk of the course – that was it. Today you have to attend seminars and be licensed and God knows what. In those days we just got on with it. Far less complicated.

'Also in that era, I ran the meeting completely on my own with no deputy. There was a chief observer who did most of the donkey work, though it was a long hard day. I started that role at Mallory Park in June 1961. The BRSCC put on saloons, 500s and eventually 5000s. We ran these mixed meetings across the season with eight or nine different races. Clive Wormleighton tried to run a balanced diary of cars and bikes but today the motorcycles are more prominent because they bring in a better gate. I had dialogues with Clive but he only really came around if we did anything that he objected to. I can't recall any particular argument with him at all. Having started in the Wormleighton era I remained at Mallory until I was forcibly retired by the MSA on 27 December 1999 on grounds of age. That was after thirty-eight years.

'Grovewood took over in 1962. John Webb was an ideas man. Fifty per cent of them were useless but the other fifty per cent were humdingers! It was him who started the Formula Ford initiative. With John his word was his bond. If he said that you had a deal he wouldn't break his word. However, he would squeeze the last farthing out of that deal. John Webb and I had a love/hate relationship for about thirty years.

Formula Vee, June 1968.

The red flag goes out as the leading trio avoid the wreck of Graham Aymes' car.

James Henderson's Morgan takes a short cut through the chicane, October 1968.

Over-1,000cc saloon race, 1969.

Dave Walker and Carlos Pace crash after their cars touch at the Esses on the last lap of the 1970 Lombank F3 race.

David Tomlinson's Elva Courier, which lost it at the exit to the chicane and struck the Armco, May 1972.

Richard Lloyd wins in March 1973.

Frank Syther – clubmans, July 1973.

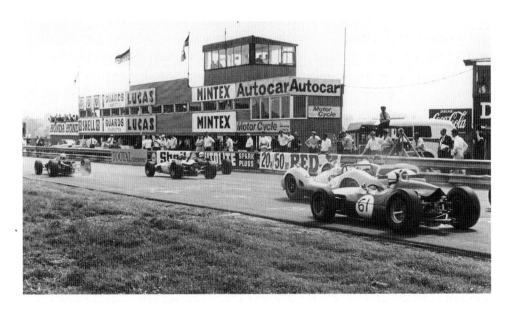

Formula Libre start, October 1968.

Number sixteen comes to rest with its petrol tank pouring its contents onto the track, July 1967.

The thing with Webby is that he is a hard-hearted little bugger but he loved his motor racing. He used to come to Mallory quite frequently, land his aircraft on the Stebbe straight, park it up in the paddock and stay there for a day's racing. You could talk motor racing with John until you were blue in the face. He used to have his little hidey-hole on top of the old pits. He used to get some of his cronies in there and they used to drag me in there occasionally for a couple of quick drinks. John was a social animal and also ran some parties on the island. Not quite as much as Chris Meek in later years, however. Webb was a driving force with vision. He would take a lot out financially but he loved his motor racing.

'With the Formula Ford I think that he had words with Walter Hayes at Ford and they cooked up Formula Ford. It took off like nobody's business. Formula Ford was more or less a replacement for Formula Three. The Formula Three was the old 500s. The 500s were international Formula Three. Formula Ford did bring on drivers.

'At Mallory I saw many famous names appear over the years. Unlike the modern Formula One era the top drivers of their day like Jim Clark, Graham Hill, Jack Brabham and John Surtees would race on alternate weekends in different formulae at tracks like Mallory Park. John Surtees made a very impressive move to four-wheel racing and was always good at Mallory in both his sports. As for Mike

F3, May 1969. In one of the closest-fought contests of the day, winner Alan Rollinson in a Brabham BT21 leads the Team Lotus S9 of Roy Pike.

Hailwood – what a smashing bloke. You wouldn't think when you were talking to him in the bar that he was what he was – which was absolutely brilliant. Surtees the same. Graham Hill was sardonic and thought it was humorous. Most people disagreed. His son, Damon, was much better. Jim Clark was a gentleman and he didn't shout about the place. Jack Brabham was a lovely bloke.

'During the Grovewood era John Webb restored the oval between the Esses and the Devil's Elbow. His idea was to get a 100mph oval so he could stage meetings on there. Of course, it didn't work out. He wanted American-style racing but he didn't get anything like the lap speeds that he wanted to make the news. It ended up as parking for breakdowns except when the Eurocars came along. When they promoted the Eurocars, they went 'the wrong way' around the circuit and they used the oval in an anti-clockwise direction.

'As for Grovewood giving up Mallory Park – I think that they had made a conscious decision that they could make more money out of Brands than they could out of Mallory. The plug was pulled. Mallory did have quite good gates but obviously not successful enough for the owners.'

As for the perspective of Bruce Widdowson: 'I first visited Mallory Park in 1962. I first came because of an involvement in motor racing and the Nottingham Sports Car Club, who actually ran the first Formula One

Damon Hill.

Damon Hill –
motorcyclist! He was
in the Yamaha RD350
Pro-Am Series.

RACE 5   Sunday, 20th September   14.30 pm

Yamaha RD350 Pro-Am Series
Round 8

THE AMS

1   NEVILLE BUSSON
2   GARY PADGETT
3   TOM DRURY
4   KEVIN MITCHELL
5   KIM BARKER
6   SIMON BEAUMONT
7   DAVID RAYBON
8   NICHOL ROBB
9   MIKE CAPON
10   DAMON HILL

The Pros

11   SIMON BUCKMASTER
12   RAY SWANN
13   PAUL BARKER
14   CONNOR BRENNAN
15   ALEX BEDFORD
16   GRAHAM ATHA
17   PETE WILD
18   PAUL HARRIS
19   ROB McELNEA
20   KEVIN ROBB
21
22   PHIL HENDERSON
23   BRENDON QUIRK

meeting, the only one that they ran at Mallory Park in 1962 as one of their regular meetings. The main race of the day was won by John Surtees from Jack Brabham, Lola and Cooper respectively. Graham Hill was a very creditable third in the four-cylinder ex-Rob Walker car. Mike Parkes was fourth but he won the GT race. Graham Hill was second in that with John Surtees third. A number of people have commented, including Peter Blaney who was the chief observer at the meeting, on how different it is to Formula One today. The drivers took part in other formulae. I think that one of the great memories of that meeting was the "Tatty Turner" of Pat Ferguson who beat all the Elites – including the Team Elite of John Wagstaff.

'I was eighteen years old and a junior marshal in those days. I used to come to the meetings in a very old, dilapidated Morris 8, which was the best that I could afford. The situation with Mallory on the marshalling side was that in the early days it was just standing on bales or concrete blocks. They had to put in marshal points hastily to a higher standard. Now they couldn't do it in time for the meeting so they made these horrible things. They were loose concrete blocks with shale in. At one meeting – although I didn't see it myself – a car did hit one and a marshal got sprayed with shale. They had to put cement in pretty quickly afterwards. Marshal facilities were obviously not as good in those days as they are now. Clothing was always ex-war surplus anoraks, which were on sale in the Army stores. The telephones were ex-Second World War field telephones. You used to get no end of static – you could hardly hear anything. It was hopeless communication.

'As for driver safety, we used to have the St John Ambulance. They would gather at one marshal point and then they would walk to another. They would eventually work their way around the circuit. Matters have improved enormously in that aspect. There was a big tree at the Esses coming uphill, which competitors have hit in the past. It has gone now, of course.

'As for attendance – like at football grounds of the period – there were huge crowds with very little control. You would get 20,000 coming to a club meeting in the 1950s because it was such a novelty. Even when I was working at club meetings at Mallory in the 1960s, you would get up to 6,000 in attendance. A lot of people used to come because motor racing was comparatively rare and live entertainment was popular. Being a marshal I never had to stand in such conditions. You could see the crowds were all squashed together. However, the viewing at Mallory is exemplary.

'The only motorcycle meeting that I've been to is the combined motorcycle and car meeting – the Plum Pudding – which I went to in 1999 as we were filming a video. I've never been to a motorcycle meeting before or since. I'm a four-wheel man.

'As I mentioned, I started off at eighteen as a course marshal. I became the second-youngest person to reach observer status in the club's history at twenty-one. When we had the 1971 race meeting for the Formula 5000 International – which was won by Mike Hailwood in a Team Surtees – I was actually the grid controller at that. It was an horrendous experience. I'll never forget it. We were standing in the start area by the quite low Armco barriers that they had. These huge Formula 5000 cars were thundering past a few feet away. You were just fixed to the spot. One or two competitors had gone off in the days when there were timber slats or bare earthworks. The car would come straight through.

'The infrastructure is very different now. There were no gravel traps in those days so if they went off at Gerard's they went straight into a bank. The changes meant it was tighter for spectators. That was purely secondary. The safety of the circuit was by far the more important. Like everywhere else, it's better than it used to be.

'When the Nottingham Sports Car Club weren't so involved at Mallory I came here with the BARC. They had a very good medical officer, Doctor Fairbrother. In those days medical facilities were very primitive. Doctor Fairbrother had a big vehicle that was the forerunner of the modern

Mike Hailwood in a Team Surtees.

rescue unit. He had his own equipment to a far higher standard than was normal.

'The Marshals' Club was founded in 1957 with great input from one of our members – Keith Douglas. It was not a big force at first. Most of the clubs provided their own marshals and their own infrastructure but some were better than others. You started off as a course marshal, which was basically assisting other marshals and making sure that spectators didn't climb over the barrier or sit on the barrier. Then you progressed to fire marshal. Fire marshals in those days had appalling training. At big race meetings the actual fire brigade were contracted to come in and provide proper facilities. However, at ordinary club meetings there were hardly any facilities for the training of marshals. It is one of the reasons that Keith Douglas and others formed the Marshals' Club.

'I started in the Wormleighton era very briefly. After the Formula One race meeting that the Nottingham Club organised, which may have enhanced the value of the circuit, Clive Wormleighton sold it to Grovewood. Nottingham Sports Car Club had one meeting a year thereafter. I came more often in the mid-1960s because of my involvement with BARC as well. These were club events and I was familiar with Mallory Park too.

'If Mallory Park had closed in 1983 it would have been a major loss. Donington had reopened nearby and that had an impact. I had very little involvement with the Overends until the late 1990s. In 1998 the NSCC celebrated its fiftieth anniversary. Chris Meek, the owner of Mallory Park, was an NSCC member in his youth and was active in car-racing meetings during the Wormleighton era and beyond. It was largely at his instigation that we actually made the videos. They build on the records that Derek Truman filmed at Mallory from 1956 to 1959 and it is good technical quality. Though there may be other footage about I can't imagine there is such a complete collection.

'Mallory Park is very much a club circuit. There is a completely different feeling there to Silverstone. While there were club meetings at Silverstone in the 1960s, it was only part and parcel of a greater happening. Of course, Mallory Park was predominantly a club circuit. With Mallory no longer staging major car events it is a circuit that does cherish its club involvement. In the Wormleighton era NSCC shared the running of car meetings with BRSSC and BARC to some extent. Nottingham was the dominant party. Clive Wormleighton did receive support from the NSCC both in terms of financial sponsorship – our main sponsors were Percy Andrews, the big dye works in Nottingham – and also work parties who helped set the circuit out. That's why I think that we had the lion's share because of the assistance that the club was able to offer. Then, of course, with Grovewood they did have a relationship with BRSCC from Brands. It was the logical thing for the BRSCC to continue. The BRSCC have been continuous from the beginning of the circuit down to the present time. Of course, the Overends were BRSCC people and I think what they achieved at the circuit under Chris Meek's ownership has been remarkable.

'Looking back, the Nottingham Sports Car Club was disappointed when Clive Wormleighton sold out after our Formula One race meeting and Grovewood reduced us to a token presence. However, we live in a commercial world where these things happen. You've got to look forward.

'My attitude was that the club had had a number of good years. A matter that a lot of people forget is that there was sympathy for the club – Timmy Brown at Silverstone with the BRDC gave us priority for all its Bank Holiday race meetings in the 1960s. It was good news that rumours started that we were going to lose Mallory Park and we actually did have a spin-off effect. There was respect for our organising ability and the NSCC was probably the most powerful regional club after the BARC and BRSCC and we did take over the primary operation at Silverstone for twelve years. Eventually the NSSC had to give up racing altogether in 1979. Ironically, Mallory Park was very sympathetic to us and offered two dates back to help us to try and keep racing. Sadly, the club couldn't run a championship for racing on two meetings. We needed four or five.

'I think that the negative memory that I have of Mallory Park from the marshalling point of view was due to the poor safety in the early days. Silverstone was well ahead of Mallory in that aspect in the 1960s. The good side at Mallory Park was that it had a much better atmosphere and the marshals were very much part of what was going on. You could also see virtually all of the circuit. If you were on Becketts – or somewhere else at Silverstone – with the wind howling around you and the snow, then you couldn't see what was going on at the rest of the circuit. The atmosphere was terrible for marshals at Silverstone but Mallory was very good.'

With Brands Hatch needing improvement owing to Formula One GP commitments, Grovewood were forced to direct more of their profits into the Kent circuit. Mallory became rather rundown and during the autumn of 1982 they finally gave up the ghost and put the circuit up for sale. Another problem for Grovewood, who had in turn been taken over by Eagle Star, was the opening of Tom Wheatcroft's fine Donington racetrack nearby, which was undoubtedly attracting major races and sponsors. There had been press analysis prior to the announcement and a link to Mr Wheatcroft himself.

Bruce Widdowson (left) with Alan Allcutt (centre) and Peter Sutcliffe (right).

Under the heading 'Owners silent over Mallory's possible sale', a local report ran: 'Directors of Grovewood Securities, the property group, were tight-lipped today about speculation that they are thinking of selling Mallory Park motor-racing circuit for housing development.

'Outline planning permission, which expires next February, exists for more than thirty houses at the circuit and this, coupled with the fact that Wigston developer Mr Bernard (Tom) Wheatcroft plans to reopen Donington Park, which is twenty miles away, for car and motorcycle racing, has given rise to the rumours. Mr Wheatcroft has been said to be interested in purchasing Mallory Park but he commented, "My interest lies purely in Donington Park, and there it is for the combined use of a museum housing my collection of racing cars and to begin racing again. I am certainly not interested in acquiring any other motor racing circuit."

'But it is understood that directors of Motor Circuit Developments, a subsidiary of Grovewood Securities who control such circuits as Mallory,

Brands Hatch and Oulton Park, have indicated they would be prepared to listen to offers for the Leicestershire circuit.

'But there was no comment from their Brands Hatch headquarters or from Mr Jim Swift, circuit manager of Mallory.

'The major shareholding in Grovewood Securities is that of the insurance concern, Eagle Star. Grovewood Securities also have interests including property, pottery and paint manufacturing.

'Mr Maurice Pettifor of the County Council Planning department confirmed that there is planning permission for a limited number of houses on the Kirkby Mallory side of the circuit. Asked if the council would consider any application for a larger number of houses on the racing circuit site, he said that no formal application had been made in this respect.'

The events following publicity like this and the eventual confirmation of the sale proved quite a saga. With planning permission for residential development and Grovewood's alleged reluctance for motor sport to continue all seemed lost. Some bidders and poseurs appeared on the scene, made various statements to the press and disappeared. Both car and motorcycle clubs, sometimes in collaboration to get a deal, did too but to no avail. With Grovewood owning other UK circuits some clubs possibly felt that by becoming involved in the purchase their position at these other circuits could be compromised. So it seemed a prophetic article that ran under 'Mallory: Is it the End?'

'Racing comes to a close at Mallory Park on Sunday, for this season at least, and when the final winner sweeps past the chequered flag in a clubman's motorcycle meeting no-one is sure whether the new owner will give the green light for it to start again next year.

'Motor Circuit Developments, who bought the circuit in 1962, have put it on the market after deciding to close the track because of falling crowd figures at the international motorcycle meetings on which it has depended, and the restricted midweek use that can be made of the circuit.

'Mr Peter Stayner, circuit director, confirmed that the transaction was out to tender and that these will be considered on 1 December, MCD retaining ownership until the end of the year.

'About a dozen individuals and groups are said to be interested in buying the circuit including Mr Tom Wheatcroft, owner of Donington Park; the British Racing and Sports Car Club and a consortium headed by Leeds millionaire racing driver Chris Meek.

'Mrs Edwina Overend, competition secretary of the BRSCC, was at the final car meeting last weekend and said that they had the money to buy the circuit and were optimistic that their bid would be accepted.

'Mallory was opened as a grass-track racing venue in the early 1950s when the national championships were held there on three occasions before it was bought by local building contractor Clive Wormleighton in July 1955.

'One of the competitors who took part in the last grass-track meeting and was to star in many international events and the Motor Cycle Sidecar Race of the Year, which he went on to win on many occasions when it became a road-racing circuit, was Mr Chris Vincent, now a motorcycle dealer in nearby Earl Shilton. He recalls: "Apart from the last grass-track meeting I took part in many of the early road ones when I first got to know Mallory. I have always had a close affinity with it and will be as sorry as anyone to see it close. I just hope here is a change of policy or plan and that racing can continue as it has given me an enormous amount of enjoyment over many years."

'Optimism is still high among all that have been associated with the circuit, not least the spectators who have patronised the meetings. Mr John Pearson of Hollydene Crescent, Earl Shilton, has been a regular on the hairpin for at least eighteen years. His wife, Sue, was introduced to Mallory during their courtship and their two sons Wayne and Ian have grown up with the sound of throbbing racing engines as familiar as anything else. He says, "It's a shame and I hope somebody does take it over and show that it can be made to pay as I don't believe crowds here are any smaller than at places like Oulton or Snetterton."

'A highlight for him over the years were the Formula 5000s and he thinks that part of the reason for the decline has been the quality of the events and competitors being of lower standard than in the past.'

A poignant moment came when Bob Gerard actually did the last lap at the final car meeting when everyone presumed it was closing, as Julian Gerard recalls: 'That was a sad day when we thought that it was all going. Bob was approaching his seventies but you could see the spark as he drove around to close it down. We got him into the car but he couldn't wear his shoes. He had quite serious gout – he suffered from that and he didn't drink. He always thought that was unfair! So he had the first lap and he had what might have been the last lap.' This was also the track on which he had won his last race in 1961.

The press coverage of the 'last race' at the motorcycle meeting dealt with both the future sale and the on-course action. First, under the heading '2,000 turn out for final event at Mallory', came this coverage: 'Nearly 2,000 people were at Mallory Park for the final meeting in the circuit's twenty-six-year history. They watched a seventeen-race programme of motorcycle races organised by the Racing 50 Motorcycle Club and run by the Midland Motorcycle Racing Club of Birmingham. Committee member of MMRC and clerk of the course Mr Mike Dawes said, "It was a very nostalgic occasion because for so many of us there, Mallory was the first circuit we ever went to. We came as boys to see cycle racing and became hooked on it. It's a great shame it has to close because it is in an ideal position from the communications point of view and has been developed to a high standard."

'As in the last car meeting the week before, rumours were rife that the circuit would – even at the eleventh hour – not be closing. Mr Dawes said, "We were told that a local industrialist had stepped in, a car club wanted to buy it and various consortiums were bidding for it." For Mr Dawes and his club this was the first meeting that they had run at Mallory and he said, "It's ironic that it should be the last event at Mallory."'

As for the 'final' action – under the headline 'Mallory's Last Winner' came the following: 'Mallory Park's last race ended at 4.12 p.m. on Sunday. And the shutters came down after twenty-six years of road racing on the 1.35-mile Leicestershire circuit with its most local winner.

'Dave East, winner of the 1981 Manx GP, came four miles from his home at Kirkby Muxloe, determined to be Mallory's last victor. He led throughout an extra ten-lap 1,000cc event to notch his twentieth Mallory victory, more than half of them scored on his MGP-winning Mk3 Suzuki-4.

'Said East: "I used to push a bike to Mallory to see Dave Croxford and John Cooper and company on their Seeleys. I've raced here since 1976 and I've won on a Velocette in the wet at Mallory."

'In the fastest of the seventeen races on the final programme, East was chased hard until halfway by Tim Lee, until his 750 Yamaha gearbox broke, and by Dave Thurlow until he slid off his 350 Yamaha at the hairpin – Mallory's last crasher!

'So the day Mallory went West, it also went East. The buzz among the shivering fans was still of past races, particularly the Cooper-Ago battle. Surprisingly few past stars turned up. Chris Vincent looked in at the scene of so many of his sidecar successes. The Motor Circuit Development men were concentrated at a Brands Hatch car meeting, but rival Donington owner Tom Wheatcroft, who wants to buy Mallory for housing, was there with former Mallory manager Tim Parnell.

'It was a sad day for racing, for there have been more good bike races at Mallory than at any other British track.

'Tender forms for the sale of Mallory's near-300 acres were posted at the weekend. In addition to Mr Wheatcroft, who lives only nine miles away from Mallory, bids are expected from a Midlands business group and from the British Racing and Sports Car Club.

Souvenir programme.

'MCD Managing Director John Webb said, "The tenders close on 26 November. Within a week of that date the buyer will be announced. There are a lot of people interested but not all of them necessarily have the money to back up their plans."'

EDWINA'S

There was plenty of media interest when the following news item appeared under the title of 'Mallory Park racing saved': 'Mallory Park motor racing circuit was bought today by Leeds businessman Mr Chris Meek for an undisclosed sum. It is hoped that motor racing will start again at the circuit in March.

'Mr Meek bought the 1.35-mile circuit, which is set in parkland and has a clubhouse and other buildings, from Grovewood Securities, a subsidiary of Eagle Star Insurance.

'It was feared that motor sport would have to end when Grovewood's operating subsidiary Motor Circuit Developments discontinued events there from October last year.

'But Mrs Edwina Overend, secretary of the Midlands Centre of the British Racing and Sports Car Club said they would be running between six and eight events at this circuit this year, and she thought there would be motorcycle races at the track.

'"There will be no championship events this year but we are going to develop the circuit for a full programme next year," she said.'

Chris Meek was profiled in an interview with the industrial editor of the *Leicester Mercury*: 'Industrialist and racing driver Mr Chris Meek, who has bought the Mallory Park racing circuit from Grovewood Securities, is confident of turning it from past substantial losses into profit this year.

'As cars and motorcycles practised for the first time this year, Mr Meek revealed plans to extend the circuit at Gerard's bend, to build another lake for fishing and the allocation of several franchises.

'The fishing rights have gone to a newly formed Leicester-based company, Mallory Park Fisheries, being operated by a group that includes Mr Roy Marlow

Motor Races

MEMBERS MEETING

Mallory Park

Sunday, 10th July, 1983

OFFICIAL PROGRAMME 30p

Programme sales in aid of the

BRITISH RACING & SPORTS CAR CLUB

A BRSCC programme from that crucial year.

and Mr Ivan Marks, which will offer what are described as "exclusive" coarse-angling facilities.

'The clubhouse at the circuit is being turned into a public house – the only one at Kirkby Mallory – and this will be run by a locally based landlord whose name is yet to be announced.

'A question mark hangs over the future use of a stable block near the paddock entrance, which has a grade two preservation order on it. Among possibilities to be considered is a conversion into a country hotel, which, including the necessary extensions, would cost about £1 million. No purchase price for the circuit has been disclosed.

'But Mr Meek wants to hear the views of local people who may have an alternative use to propose for this building. "We have a number of other ideas in mind that would really put Mallory Park on the map. Our main concern is that the 300-acre park must be made viable, that projects should be acceptable to the planning authorities and that the needs and well-being of the residents of Kirkby Mallory are a high priority," said Mr Meek.

'The car and racing franchise is being operated by the British Racing and Sports Car Club.'

This was following the positive announcement that 'Mallory Gets Official OK': 'After circuit inspections by the Royal Automobile Club and the Auto Cycle Union – motor sport's governing bodies – Mallory Park has been given the go-ahead to hold race meetings this year.

'In granting the permit for motor racing, the RAC's Robert Langford complimented circuit staff on the speedy way that essential track work was being done. And the ACU confirmed several motorcycle race dates between June and October. Meanwhile, £10 season tickets are being bought by enthusiasts as far away as Ireland.

'Circuit manager Mrs Edwina Overend says: "As more and more clubs request dates for meetings, the season passes look to be bigger and better bargains. We offered the season passes at a low price when funds were urgently required for essential track work and were amazed at the response from enthusiasts.

'"But we intend to hold the price for this year, so people will be entitled to attend every meeting this year. Fifteen have already been confirmed for only £10 – that's got to be the bargain of the season," said Mrs Overend.'

That was the fans' reaction, but how about the general community? 'Mallory is Part of Our Heritage' was a welcome headline. The article read:

'Reactions to the sale of Mallory Park to Yorkshire businessman Mr Chris Meek included a general "OK" for motor sports and a warm reception for other activities like water sports, athletics, and cycling that could be introduced.

Left: Cyclists.

Below: A Penny-farthing!

'Some even enthused about the prospect like farmer Mr Robert Spence, whose only worry was that Mr Meek might be swayed in his intentions by others in the village. He said the track was past the village and he was delighted to have motor sport back. "I have been born and bred in the village. I have lived here all my life, and it is part of our image, part of our heritage," he said.

'He welcomed the other possible development, saying that it was a pity to have a large tract of land lying unused.

'Others were more reserved in their acceptance of renewed motor racing, like mother of three Mrs Julie Bee. She said, "As long as it is not going to be excessively noisy, and as long as the police are able to control the traffic – which bothers us more than anything because often you cannot get in or out of the village – then it does not worry me too much."

'Mrs Elsie Heath, from Barwell Road, did not think the changes would make much difference to the village, although like Mrs Bee and others she stressed that she would not want engine noise every day.

'And shopkeeper Mrs Valerie Ball said, "It sounds OK to me. I do not mind the racing over the circuit anyway. My husband was born in the village and we knew when we came here that it was here. Obviously with keeping a shop it was advantageous to us."

'She said the other sports that could materialise sounded great. "They've got the lakes and everything and it is a shame they are not being used," she said. "It would not be so far for the children to go if they wanted to do something like that."

'Peckleton Parish Council chairman Mr Ken Brown welcomed the idea and said the fear had been that the park would end up being used for housing and be turned into a great big building site. He was sure people preferred sports. "At least the news that it will be retained as a sports complex is good," he said, "Motor racing will not really affect anybody because it has always been here."'

Edwina Overend gave the following perspective on the work ahead under the title 'So Glad to be in Action Again': 'Mallory Park roared back to life this week when the gates were opened for the first official practice since its October closure.

'There were no great crowds to herald its new awakening, but the first visitors, drivers and riders were happy to renew their acquaintance with "The Friendly Circuit," even in disgusting weather. They were just glad to be back.

'The familiar rising wail of accelerating machines and the zip as they sped past race control at once wiped out the question mark that hung over Mallory's racing future when the park was first put up for sale. Now there is no doubt. Practices will take place every Wednesday. The first meeting – for cars – will be held, if the fates permit, on 29 May. And by 1985 the circuit could be seeing again the international events that once made it famous.

Chris Meek.

'Organising the racing will be Mallory Park 1983 Ltd, the new subsidiary company set up by the British Racing and Sports Car Club, which negotiated full rights to that side of things with new owner Mr Chris Meek.

'Manager of the company is BRSCC competitions secretary, Mrs Edwina Overend, who keeps a soft spot in her heart for the Mallory circuit as the place where she became hooked on motor sports.

'It was to Mallory that she first went as a spectator, and there that she was originally cajoled into acting as a marshal. She later took her post with the BRSCC and in that role was a frequent visitor to the circuit. Now she is commuting daily from her Lichfield home. She will have to cope with the day-to-day running of the circuit, the bookings, the paperwork and the organisation.

'Re-opening the circuit is also an expensive job, for she says virtually nothing has been left behind. The medical centre is bare and needs to be equipped with everything from bandages to resuscitation equipment and the cutting gear to free drivers from crashed cars. There are flags and other items of circuit furniture to be bought, along with fire extinguishers and masses of tyres that need to be banded together for protection. Many have disappeared since the last event.

'Helping to change the face of the forlorn-looking track is circuit foreman Mr Alan Hodgkinson, a dedicated man from the old days of the circuit who says Mrs Overend arrives early, leaves late and "never looks at a clock".

'She hopes to secure events of national standing as part of a full 1984 programme and she fully intends Mallory to be back in the big time come 1985.'

Chris Meek in track action.

What of the colourful new owner Chris Meek? Chris achieved over 500 wins during his racing career. These embraced all kinds of single-seater racing, including Formula Two, Formula Atlantic, Formula Libre, Formula Ford, Formula Three, Saloons, Special Saloons, Sports Racing and GT cars. Chris also gained the highest number of lap records of any other driver, many of which were at Mallory Park. He was seven-times production car champion, being virtually unbeatable in the 1970s and 1980s. As works driver with Elva Cars in the early 1960s, he succeeded in breaking the domination of the Lotus Elite, and continued to head the Elva team when they moved into single-seaters. However, with the development of his business, Chris was unable to devote himself full-time to Elva, and they parted company on amicable terms. Chris then joined Ginetta as works driver, where he was more easily available to combine his commercial and racing activities. Chris won many races for the team.

Chris's Formula Two activities were pursued with Bill Jones' Shardlow International Racing Organisation during the late 1960s. He drove a Brabham with much success. Chris enjoyed innumerable racing successes at the wheels of a variety of high-performance production cars. Notable among these were his wins with Count Condivi's de Tomaso Pantera. In 1974 he joined Colin

Chris Meek's first racing car – the JBS Jap Brough.

Chapman to drive a Dealer Team Lotus Europa, a car in which he was almost unbeatable. In fact, Chris was to win more races for Lotus than any other driver. So Mallory Park had become the property of an enthusiastic, highly motivated motor sport participant, whose trophy room bore witness to the success that he had enjoyed on the circuits.

What of the perspective of the man himself? 'My first love was racing motorcycles. After my first series of broken bones my interest in racing cars was born. During a visit to the Charterhall circuit I met up with Jock McBain, who persuaded me to purchase his F3 500cc JBS Jap. My first race was in 1957. That was the first year that I visited Mallory Park. I was excited and thrilled at the circuit's setting among the trees, also the warm atmosphere surrounding the activities of this new venue. Driving was a real challenge, such fun with unprotected trees, corners and banking. Of course, the excitement of managing a third place overall was the pinnacle against superior opposition in the form of new models.

'After driving the car to and from the meeting as we did in those days, third overall in the sports car race driving an ex-Anstead Brown 1,172cc Lotus Mk 9 was an extreme contrast and much more of a challenge than racing on the many aerodrome circuits throughout England at the time, such as Charterhall, Rufforth and Full Sutton.

'Of my subsequent hundreds of wins and places, I have to say that one of the most satisfying came ten years after my first visit to Mallory Park. This was winning two races for Ginetta Cars Ltd, driving their new and untested first rear-engined 1,600cc G12 GT car. I remember winning the GT race and then the Formula Libre race starting from the back of the grid. Drivers' favourite Don Truman was in charge on that occasion and is still synonymous with Mallory Park to the present day.

'As for my overall career aspirations as a driver, racing for me was always just a bit of fun. I had offers from some of the big boys in the early days but I always enjoyed being the underdog. My acquisition of Mallory Park came down to heart – everything connected with cars, motorcycles and racing is always ruled by the heart.

'When I first acquired the estate I was approached by a planning officer (an attractive lady) to consider extending the village into the estate. She mentioned that planning approval had already been granted and indeed footings were already in place for housing. I insisted that irrespective of financial gain my wish was to protect the unencumbered motor racing planning approval activities. In the beginning of our ownership Mallory Park was treated as a hobby and heavily subsidised.

'My happiest memories of being involved as circuit owner are of partying on my little island – Fantasy Island. It was once the preserve of the rich and famous, the abode of the privileged few. Dignitaries would land their planes on Stebbe Straight, holding up practice and racing, then partying until the early hours of the following morning. Having never received an invitation, in jest I recall saying to my friends that one day I will own this estate and you are all invited. Over the years we did have fabulous parties, with fond memories of Roger Clark and his family always being the life and soul of the party.

'Apart from motor racing and partying on my little island, I also enjoy walking the several hundred acres of our estate. This is full of wildlife in all its forms including badgers, foxes, hares, stoats, water voles and in and around our seven lakes are kingfishers, herons, cormorants, rare ducks and geese. We have several families of nesting owls and an abundance of rare plants, wild flowers and ancient trees. We try to protect all of this and do not allow any hunting or shooting on the estate.'

What of the Overend family, whose subsequent management of the arena certainly reinforced the reputation as 'The Friendly Circuit'? Mallory Park had also appeared on the horizon long before the events of 1983, as Ron Overend explains: 'Our interest in motor sport came through my son David, really. When he was about ten he was very interested in motor sport. We used to go to various tracks and I remember that we went to Mallory when it was pouring with rain. I think that was in 1967, a meeting that John Surtees won.

Fantasy Island.

'We used to take in a bit of rallying, David and I. At that time the BRSCC
– which I was later involved with – had a rescue unit that used to go out on
the rallying during the winter. We met up and chatted, with this ending up with
our going over to Mallory. We used to wander around Mallory Park in 1967
and 1968, gradually getting involved. In fact I took over the rescue vehicle at
Mallory Park, looking after that for a while in the late 1960s. Then I went on
and undertook various jobs for the BRSCC. In 1969 I was asked to become
competitions secretary but at the time I was in business so Edwina decided to
take it on. She had been involved at Mallory – at the start line and on the boards.
I continued in my business until after we had taken Mallory Park over. I tried

Chris and friends would
love you to join in the
fun at our Garden Party
on **'Fantasy Island'**

Buffet — Bar B-Q — Drinks
from 12.30 p.m.

Dress As You Please

R.S.V.P.
Please reply to:
TITAN GROUP
Titan House
P.O. Box HH22
Leeds LS8 2UY
Tel: (0532) 490444

P.T.O.

Fantasy Island.

The Overend family.

to carry on initially but it was starting to get busy as she had built the circuit's business up quite a bit. I used to go over there part-time but by 1987 I went over there full time. It was quite a transition from spectating to running the circuit.

'We were always interested in cars but we were not into the motorcycle scene at all. People tended to warn us off the bikers but in reality we found them a most charming set. They were no different from the car fraternity. Basically it is motor sport racing. We got on with them excellently. We built up a good understanding with them. They helped us a lot initially – especially Mark Jessup and his family. We were four-wheel orientated and then we got involved with both. The situation with Mallory is that although they run car racing there, bike racing is the main activity. They run the big bike meetings and lots of practice. In fact when we took the circuit over there was a lot of hoo-haa and rubbish talked about what we could do and what we couldn't do.

'As I mentioned, Edwina helped out the BRSCC a bit on the start line. When I was in business she was basically a housewife. Anyway, she took over as competitions secretary. She ran it very well because the thing with her was that she got to know all the drivers and everybody else. They all knew her and would ring her up about entries. It all went very well. Of course, on the Mallory side, when we took over the circuit had become very run-down from the late 1970s. Obviously they didn't want to invest the money. Then Donington opened up just down the road, which was a magnificent circuit. I think that Grovewood, who were the owners, felt that was the final straw. They put it on the market. Then there were all sorts of people coming and going who were promising to do this and that. Edwina approached Chris Meek, who had been a top driver, an excellent driver. Very competitive and very experienced. She chatted to him about it and he said that he would have a look at it. Anyway, he did finally purchase the site. Of course, he knew Mallory and thought that it was just the racetrack. Well the Mallory Estate is coming on for 300 acres. When it was confirmed that he had got it and he came down and had another look, he said, "I didn't realise that it was all this." He knew that he had got a bargain. Chris was an identikit owner. He had strong Mallory links, he had motor sport at heart and was wealthy. He is a substantial property owner. He is interested and understands the sport.

'The arrangement that Edwina made with him was that he would buy it and we would lease it, initially for the first few months through the BRSCC. After a few months we thought that we would drive the ship ourselves. We took it over and we signed a new lease in 1984 and formed a new company, Mallory Park Motor Sport Ltd.

'When we took it over we were told by a lot of folk that we were mad, that we would be bankrupt in six months. We were told how foolish we were. So Edwina became so determined that she just pushed it and pushed it. Initially we were told that we couldn't run many meetings because that was the agreement with the local authority. She said to me, "Well, I think that our best thing to do is put the maximum number of meetings on." So in 1983, because we were trying to get clubs to come into the circuit we only ran about fifteen meetings. By 1985 she put seventy meetings on! So then we had an approach from the Hinckley and Bosworth Environmental Department saying, "Look here, what's this all about?" So we said that there was no agreement, for we had found that out already. So they said that they would like to draw up an agreement with us to limit matters. They stated that they appreciated that we were running a business. We said okay and sat down with them. For 1985 and 1986 it was actually a noise control order – it wasn't a planning agreement. There were no planning restrictions on Mallory Park when it was originally built by Clive Wormleighton. But they could serve a nuisance order so we did an agreement with them. It was all done very amicably as they understood that we were running a business. The agreement for the first two years was that we would run forty-five meetings and then we would run forty meetings a year. This is every weekend except in the close season, when you cannot run. Plus we would run a limited amount of midweek activity, a limited amount we were happy with. So there were midweek days including one day of practice. We also agreed with them to be able to run on Saturday for the racing schools on a lower noise level. So that's how we finished up. It was a good mix in reality.

'The big problem was, of course, that you really had to have a couple of days' working around the track. What we did was that the Mondays after the race meetings were used for clearing up. There was not a lot of clearing up after bike meetings but after car meetings where they had hit the barriers, all that had to be replaced. On the Friday before the meeting at the weekend it was a case of getting everything ready. It was quite a stretch. We could probably have done with more time. We were running meetings and we needed them to bring in money for our company. It became a big commitment for the family. David was an accountant in Birmingham. About 1988 we chatted to him about it and he started looking after the accounts. Then just after that we said, "What about joining the company?" So he came over. By 1990 we were running it completely as a family. David was well into motor sport and he injected quite a few new ideas. I must say that it went well. He brought back the big meetings – the Post-TT and the Race of the Year. He persuaded the riders to attend. One of the major problems we had when we took over was the fact that British Touring Cars and all those major car races weren't coming any more. The people who owned Brands owned other circuits too. They put these events to their circuits and I can't blame them. We would have done the same, I expect. So we knew that bikes – which had been a big attraction at Mallory – were the events to concentrate on, which we did.

Post-TT cover.

Joey Dunlop – a popular competitor
in the Race of the Year.

Everyman's.

Above left: Drayton Croft School.

Above right: EMRA

'Gradually Edwina brought in two racing schools – Everyman and a Suzuki bike school. The latter was run by Drayton Croft, the local motorcycle dealers. When we first started we had an approach from a car racing school. Then he sold out to John Farnham and John built it into a major business. John took over in 1990.

'Going back to our launch, it was tough getting the diary sorted. The motor sport calendar is usually done about June or July of the year before. There are hiccups when international meetings are altered, which makes matters difficult. Yes, it was difficult. There are some who claim that Mallory Park closed down. In fact it never closed down. It was sold in 1982 and ran virtually to the end of 1982. Then we took it over and in May 1983 we ran our first car meeting. It was the 750 club and that was followed by the Retford Club the following week on bikes. The BRSCC came in running meetings and the ACU – it is split into various areas – their Midland area, which is the East Midlands ACU formed a club. The East Midlands Racing Association more or less took over the bulk of the club-bike racing plus some of the bigger events. So by July 1983 we were already negotiating with clubs for the following year. So by 1984 we were back onto forty-five meetings.

1. The Mallory family insignia.

2. The late, great Mike Hailwood on the track.

3. John Surtees and family.

4. Hazel and Clive Chapman with Chris Meek recall the Lotus triumphs.

5. *Above:* Edwina with Chris Meek and his 208, Mallory Park, 1978.

6. *Right:* Edwina with Jamie Whitham (left) and John Reynolds (right), 1992 Supercup.

7. Edwina with Phil Read, Jim Redman and Giacomo Agostini, Post-TT 1995.

8. Edwina with Randy Mamola and riders for the Health Charity event.

9. Gareth Wills – the winner of the Edwina Overend Memorial Trophy, 2004. Abie Overend (Edwina's granddaughter) is on the left.

10. A Ferrari at Mallory Park.

11. In hot pursuit!

12. A closely fought race.

13. Vintage racing at Mallory Park.

14. A car of yesterday.

15. Taking the inside line.

16. Renaults.

17. Fords.

18. Minis.

19. Citroens.

20. Matters of concern for Mike Hailwood and John Surtees.

21. A busy time for Team Surtees.

22. Keeping an eye on the competition?

23. Sammy Miller with his V4 supercharged AJS.

24. Sammy Miller and the streamlined NSU Sportsmax.

25. Randy Mamola (left), Will Hartog (centre) and Gary Crosby (right).

26. Race day atmosphere.

27. *Above:* Local lad Ray Stringer in spectacular action.

28. *Left:* Steve Hislop, outright lap-record holder, on a Devimead Ducati 916 Corsa.

29. *Right:* Chris Walker.

30. *Below:* Troy Bayliss.

31. Jim Moodie.

32. Race action.

'In 1983 there was definite activity and I remember that Edwina was organising practice from the end of February and into early March 1983. So the circuit moved into use then we agreed noise levels with the local authority. The governing bodies of the sport give details negotiated with the Government's Department of the Environment. Councils accept that is what it is. So we agreed those noise levels with them. That was it and we went from there. The working relationship with the village was very good. As well as being competition secretary of the BRSCC, towards the end of the closures Edwina did look after the circuit. She managed it for a year. So she got contacts with local people. I must say that she was very friendly and had a lot of friends in the village. When we first went to address the villagers through meetings it did get contentious at times but otherwise it was okay. The situation with Kirkby Mallory is that the majority of residents have only moved in since the circuit has been open. When you move in you know that there is a circuit there.

'Of course, Edwina was popular locally. She was in the WI and the local scrabble club in the village. She attended events at the church such as harvest festivals. So she knew a lot of people. What eventually happened was that, instead of villagers phoning up the council and moaning about the noise and saying that we were not supposed to be running on a particular day, they would phone her up instead. She would tell them that we were not running anything that day and invite them up to see. It was either a farmer bringing in his hay or someone on a back road on a motorbike. We had a very good relationship with the villagers. I don't know the present proprietors of the little village shop but we were very friendly with those who ran it before. They told us that well over fifty per cent of their business came through the racetrack. Since Everyman had the workshops there, along have come other concerns to whom Chris Meek's company has let premises. Of course they go up and down to the shop for their cigarettes and snacks. It does keep the shop very busy.

'The villagers were also our eyes and ears. With our security on the gate visitors had to show a pass and then they would let them in. Edwina would get phone calls telling us that there was a car with such and such a registration –"and we have just seen them open the boot and someone has climbed in." Or "There is a caravan and I've just seen three people get out of the car and lie on the floor of the caravan." When they got to the gate they were so surprised to be challenged – "How did you know?" they would ask.

'Edwina carried on right up to 2003. In fact we did several major jobs there, including a new medical centre, which was a substantial undertaking. We put the new corner in for motorbikes, which is known as "Edwina's". The cars have used it but the rumble strips that the cars wanted put in the bikes were not very happy with. So at the moment it stands that only bikes use it. Then we finally built the new race control and hospitality suite area. The offices were about the last project that we did. She saw me put in the footings for it. There is a photograph taken in October 2003, which is in the Byron Suite, of her presenting the cup to Michael Rutter for his victory in the Race of the Year. She was really struggling. She passed away in the November.

'A lot of the top names cut their teeth at Mallory Park. She knew them all because she signed them on and dealt with them. You've got Nigel Mansell and Emerson Fittipaldi who come to mind in the cars. Jonathan Palmer, who owns Brands Hatch, was a lap record holder. Ayrton Senna was another who came through and David Coulthard in more recent times. If ever we had social occasions, such as with the MSA when they have all the top people there, they would come over and chat. She had that personality. She knew everybody and their wives. She knew all their children's names. When they signed on she would ask, "How is little Billy getting on?" They were taken by the fact that she could remember these personal details.

'With the two-wheel scene she knew John Cooper, who is a legend around Mallory, plus Barry Sheene, of course. When he did finish his bike racing he took up touring cars for a couple of years for Mazda. We saw him again then. He also came back to Mallory for the Post-TT when we ran it as a classic event and brought the former riders over.

'The last time that I saw him was at a practice session on a Wednesday before a big classic meeting at Donington. That was 2001 as I recall. I spotted him in the café at the circuit having lunch. We had a chat and I remarked, "Don't forget to call in and see Edwina." Barry replied, "You needn't worry, I shall certainly call in and see her." Which he did. Within less than a year Barry had passed away.

'Clive Wormleighton had created the Post-TT and the Race of the Year. David revived these in the early nineties. When Clive and John Webb ran the Post-TT, they ran it as a modern meeting. We knew that we couldn't get the riders from the Grand Prix and the Superbikes to come to Mallory Park for events – so David turned it into a Classic event. It has been very successful. We were able to attract household names – Agostini, Phil Read, Barry Sheene etc. We brought riders such as Gary Nixon and Dave Aldana over from the States. These all attracted good crowds. However, the crowds at Mallory weren't what they were in the old days, in Clive's day and John Webb's day. Once the Sunday Shopping Act came in they dropped even further. People would say to me that we were ever so busy on Sunday as there were hundreds of cars going our way. I would tell them that they were on the way to the garden centre up the road! The crowds did build up for a big meeting and with the Race of the Year we could usually manage a sprinkling of top names.

Michael Rutter.

Emerson Fittipaldi – F3 winner, August 1969.

BRSCC ⬡

BRITISH
SALOON CAR CHAMPIONSHIP MEET.

MALLORY PARK   Sunday 22nd March 1981

To: Mrs. Edwina Overend, BRSCC, Mallory Park, Kirkby Mallory, Leicestershire.

ENTRY FORM

PLEASE USE A SEPARATE FORM FOR EACH CAR AND WRITE IN BLOCK CAPITALS

Name of Entrant ......Van Diemen International Racing Service Ltd.

Full Address ....

.........................Tel. No. (Home)...............(Bus)..........

Entrant's Licence No. ....Club and Memb. No. ....

Name of Driver .. Ayrton de Silva ....

Full Address ...... as above ....

.........................Tel. No. (Home)...............(Bus)..........

Driver's home town.. Sao Paulo, Brazil ..Club and Memb. No. ....

Competition Licence No. ....Grade.................

Make of Car Van Diemen ....Year .. 1981 .Type (model) .. RF81 ..

Make of engine . Minister ....No. of cylinders.....4....c.c. 1600

I wish to enter Race No.. 4 ...for .. FFord Cars in class ....

Has the driver raced before ☑Yes ☐No, at this circuit before ☐Yes ☑No

Does the driver wish to have his Race Licence signed ☑Yes ☐No

If you are the holder of a permanent number please enter this below, failure may result in you acc...ng a number allocated by the organisers.

No entry will be accepted unless accompanied by the correct entry fee. Cheques should be made payable to the BRSCC and please add your Cheque Card number on the back of your cheque.

The declaration on the reverse side must be completed and signed.

PERMANENT NUMBER	2 6	FOR OFFICIAL USE ONLY		
	DATE RECEIVED	DATE ACKNOWL	ENTRY FEE	COMP. NUMBER
	26 JAN 1980	26 JAN 1980	£2 100 4 ENTRIES	3
			SIGN	

Ayrton Senna's entry form.

DECLARATION:

"I have read the supplementary regulations issued for this event and agree to be bound by them and by the General Regulations of the RAC British Motor Sports Association Ltd. In consideration of the acceptance of this entry or of my being permitted to take part in this event, I agree to save harmless and keep indemnified the RAC British Motor Sports Association Ltd., such person, persons or body as may be authorised by the RAC British Motor Sports Association Ltd., to promote or organise this event and their respective officials, servants, representatives and agents from and against all actions, claims, costs, expenses and demands in respect of death or injury to myself howsoever caused arising out of or in connection with this entry or my taking part in this event, and notwithstanding that the same may have been contributed to or occasioned by the negligence of the said bodies, their officials, servants, representatives or agents.

Furthermore, in respect of any parts of this event on ground where third party insurance is not required by the law this agreement shall in addition to the parties named above extend to all and any other competitor/s and their servants and agents and to all actions, claims, costs, expenses and demands in respect of loss or damage to the person or property of myself, my driver(s), passenger(s) or mechanic(s).

'My age is . . . .(if applicable state ''Over 17 years'')'

I declare that to the best of my belief the driver(s) possess(es) the standard of competence necessary for an event of the type to which this entry relates and that the vehicle entered is suitable and roadworthy for the event having regard to the course and the speeds which will be reached.

I understand that should I at the time of this event be suffering from any disability whether permanent or temporary which is likely to affect prejudicially my normal control of my vehicle, I may not take part unless I have declared such disability to the RAC British Motor Sports Association Ltd. who have, following such declaration, issued a licence which permits me to do so.

I undertake that at the time of the event to which this entry relates, I shall be in possession of a current Medical Certificate.''

Signature of Entrant . .

Signature of Driver . . .

Date . . . . .I enclose Cheque/Postal Order. . . . .

Cheque Card No. . . . .

IMPORTANT: Any indemnity and/or declaration as prescribed by the paragraphs above which is signed by a person under the age of 18 shall be countersigned by that person's parent or guardian, whose full name and address shall be given below.

Name of Parent/Guardian . . . .

Full Address. . . . .

. . . .

. . . .

Signature of Parent/Guardian . . . .

Ayrton Senna's entry form.

'Club meetings were the bread and butter of the business with the extra of a few big hits. We wanted to do that and the good opportunity for us was when the British Superbikes were formed and were televised. Before that we ran the Supercup, which was a national championship featuring some big riders. The Superbikes is a very professional set-up. It is high profile and the manufacturers are involved. That always brings a reasonable crowd. The riders like the circuit because it is challenging. At the 2005 Superbikes I was over there and they did have quite a few accidents. They were nudging each other and coming off at Edwina's Corner, which was a bit tricky for them at the start. There were comments from the riders.

'One of the big problems is that you undertake work and then you get criticism for it. A lot, of course, is undertaken for their safety. In 1998 we put in what is known as the Bus Stop chicane because the bikes were going so fast, with the speed increasing each year. So we put that in to slow them down. After four years they were above the speed they were doing before we put it in. Then a couple of years ago they were very worried about the lap times because the

British Racing & Sports Car Club Limited

MIDLAND CENTRE

Commentator's Information Sheet

The co-operation of competitors in completing this form is greatly appreciated

DATE OF MEETING 1ST MAY EVENT No. 7 COMPETITION No. 6

A. DRIVER:

Surname COULTHARD   Christian name usually used DAVID

Occupation .... Age 18   Home Town TWYNHOLM

Previous experience and success: Six years Karting experience : Two 1st places and a 5TH place from the first three rounds of the chmps

B. CAR:

Make VAN DIEMEN Model RF89   Date 1089

Chassis and body modifications NONE

ENGINE:

Make (if different from above) FORD 1600cc

Make of conversion SCHOLAR

Previous ownership and history

Additional notes:

Please hand this form in to the Secretary of the Meeting at signing on.

Commentator's information sheet on David Coulthard.

Race 2 & 7 Dunlop Autosport Star of Tomorrow FF1600 Championship

No.	Entrant	Hometown	Car	Engine	C.C.
1	Jonathan Lewis Racing with Mobil 1	Tamworth	Van Diemen RF89 Minister Driver: Kelvin Burt		1600
2	Jonathan Lewis Racing/Mobil 1	Richmond	Van Diemen RF89 Minister Driver: Russell Spink		1600
3	Jonathan Lewis Racing with Mobil 1	Hull	Van Diemen RF89 Minister Driver: Jonathan Moore		1600
4	Jonathan Lewis Racing/Mobil 1	Bracknell	Van Diemen RF89 Minister Driver: David Goode		1600
5	Jonathan Lewis Racing/Mobil/Anderson	Liverpool	Van Diemen RF89 Minister Driver: Brian Anderson		1600
6	Team Eternit	Twynholm	Van Diemen RF89 Scholar Driver: David Coulthard		1600
7	Cubitt Builders & Plant Hire	Eye, Suffolk	Van Diemen RF89 Scholar Driver: George Cubitt		1600
8	Foundation Racing	London	Van Diemen RF89 Auriga Driver: Lyndon Barrett		1600
9	Electrotech Control Design Services	Kidlington	Reynard FB89 Scholar Driver: Graham Fennymore		1600
10	Tele Nova with Brands Hatch Racing	Orpington	Van Diemen RF88 Minister Driver: Chris Goodwin		1600
11	Dunkirk Metals Ltd	Nottingham	Van Diemen RF88 Scholar Driver: Paul Waine		1600
12	Jason Weller	Bognor Regis	Van Diemen RF88 Scholar		1600
14	Sonic Racing	Manchester	Van Diemen RF89 Scholar Driver: Matt Aitken		1600
15	Julian Pitocco	Torquay	Van Diemen RF88 Ford		1600
16	Olympic Motorsport	Ongar	Van Diemen RF88 Minister Driver: Chris Boocock		1600
17	John Wilcock	Dronfield	Mantis JL89 N Brown		1600
18	David Lloyd	Corfe Castle	Van Diemen RF88 Connaught		1600
19	Venom Racing Services	Taunton	Van Diemen RF89 Scholar Driver: Adrian Coles		1600
20	Dave Greenwood Motorsport	Weybridge	Van Diemen RF88 Scholar Driver: Graham Reed		1600
21	David Sears Motorsport	London	Van Diemen RF89 Scholar Driver: Harry Nuttall		1600
22	Amity Racing	Ashby	Reynard 89FF Scholar Driver: Scott Lakin		1600
23	Sonic Racing	London	Van Diemen RF89 Scholar Driver: Terry Fullerton		1600
24	Performance Eng. Services	Kenilworth	Van Diemen RF89 P.E.S. Driver: Steve Deeks		1600
25	Richard Fores	Chalfont	Van Diemen Scholar		1600
26	GT Services	Solihull	Swift FB88 G.T.S. Driver: Richard Shaw		1600
27	Revo Racing	London	Swift FB89 DAD Driver: Robert Verdon-Roe		1600
28	Woodcock Bros/Kurt Luby Motorsport	Ashtead	Van Diemen RF88 Auriga Driver: Garry Woodcock		1998
29	Anthony Hampsheir	Dartford	Eldon MK 27 Searle Driver: Anthony Hampsheir		1600

David Coulthard is listed driving for Team Eternit (No. 6).

Superbikes were getting faster and faster. So we put Edwina's corner in – so levelling off the Esses. There was a bit of a dip in that so we straightened that out. That took about 4 seconds a lap off the lap times. When we put it in, before we did anything we were instructed. You can't put amendments in willy-nilly. The governing bodies licence the track and they inspect it. If there are any safety problems that have come up in the previous year then they have to be resolved, of course.

Above: Glen Richards.

Left: John Reynolds in action.

Opposite: John Reynolds.

'We put it in and Michael Rutter and Glen Richards both tested it. The cars tested it too. The Everyman people have got regular race drivers who instruct and they seemed very happy with it. We ran a car meeting with it and there were a few problems, mainly because the work had just been done. When they ran off the track they were picking up gravel and all sorts of stuff. The grass hadn't grown so this was then dragged back on the track, causing problems. There is talk of trying to slow them down further – possibly as they come out of Gerard's. The cars don't use the chicane or Edwina's at the moment. Obviously they can be considerably faster than the motorbikes. The lap record is around 39 seconds, which is an average speed, including the hairpin, of 125mph. The bikes, with the top riders, are lapping at around 101mph, which is about 47 seconds. John Reynolds was the first man to break 100mph on a bike at the circuit. Edwina was very worried about riders and safety. If there was a serious crash she would get so upset about it. It's a great sport but that side of it spoils it. However, she said that she would put a grand up if someone breaks it. We thought that we would be safe for a while but John Reynolds broke it in a Supercup meeting. At that meeting three or four others broke it as well. John was the first so he won the £1,000.

'In 2003 we amalgamated the Race of the Year to run alongside the Superbike meeting because we knew that we would get all the top riders in. John Reynolds, who won the Championship as well, he won that race. We had put a thousand

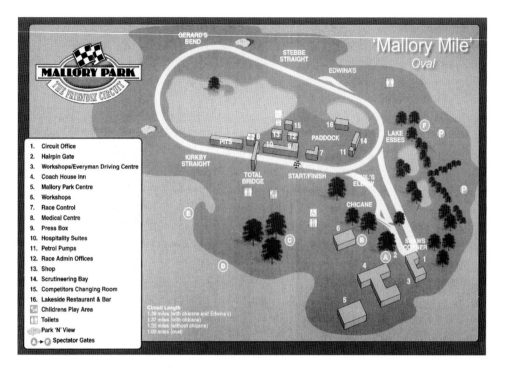

1. Circuit Office
2. Hairpin Gate
3. Workshops/Everyman Driving Centre
4. Coach House Inn
5. Mallory Park Centre
6. Workshops
7. Race Control
8. Medical Centre
9. Press Box
10. Hospitality Suites
11. Petrol Pumps
12. Race Admin Offices
13. Shop
14. Scrutineering Bay
15. Competitors Changing Room
16. Lakeside Restaurant & Bar
    Childrens Play Area
    Toilets
    Park 'N' View
    Spectator Gates

Circuit Length
1.39 miles (with chicane and Edwina's)
1.37 miles (with chicane)
1.35 miles (without chicane)
1.00 miles (oval)

Mallory Oval.

quid on that. So I was presenting him with another £1,000 and telling him that I was fed up of having to keep coughing up money when I saw him! Actually, he is a very nice guy so I wasn't too unhappy.

'As to other activities, when we took over we had an approach from Roy Marlow, who had a big shop in Leicester and was well up in a fishing organisation. So we leased the lakes to him. In fact he's made it very successful. There were already four lakes in the park area and he built another just outside. It was still on the circuit's land. It's busy and no issue about noise! I wonder why they sit there sometimes with a race meeting going on because you are supposed to ruminate. I presume with fishing you sit there and think all day.

'Before we took over, the lakes were run with surfing and speedboat racing. What we discovered was that the speedboats, in particular, eroded the edges of the lakes. With the one corner – especially Gerard's – running quite close to the end of the lake, which we had to build up and protect, we decided to stop that. Also, when you have a very well-organised fishing club you cannot have boats. Roy took it over and it is just run for fishing all the year around.

'We've also run karts. When we first took Mallory over we put kart meetings on the track. Grovewood actually had a kart track within the paddock but we

A tank.

A quad.

A buggy.

took that out and we built a kart track overlooking the circuit on a site towards the church. We developed that into a non-race track.

'We also had motocross and four-wheel driving in the area. Everyman then put a kart track in and had karts plus quads. John Farnham also obtained these two tanks from Russia and they were very popular. We did have a bit of trouble with these because when they started them up you couldn't see for about ten minutes with all the smoke! The motocross circuit is still used but it is not for competition. It is used as a leisure and practice facility. We did try to use it for racing but it didn't go very well. Also we were using four-wheel drives and quads on it, which would churn it up. We also had some ditches put in and they didn't suit the bikes.

'With respect to the Transatlantic races, Edwina ran the last one for Chris Lowe in 1981. They were popular. We tried to put it back on. We spoke to Donington, whom we have got great relations with. Tom Wheatcroft proved a very good friend of ours. We proposed to put it on between us on consecutive days. It was originally three meetings at Brands Hatch, Mallory Park and Oulton Park. Costs were prohibitive. Looking at crowd levels, people do exaggerate the old levels terrifically. They talk of 60,000 at Mallory Park. You have a job handling 15,000. There are health and safety issues to take on board today. You have to do a lot more thinking about toilet and car parking ratios for instance.

'Looking back on favourite memories: with respect to the cars we ran this series called the Eurocars with Philip Bond of Incarace. They ran the opposite way around, which was all a bit thrilling. They were excellent meetings and brought good crowds. The cars were built by Sunny Howard, who had constructed a lot of vehicles for stock car racing on short circuits. He originally had the idea along with Philip Bond and they wanted to put it onto circuit racing. We were the only track with an oval at the time. The other one since is Rockingham. We decided that we would put it on and went for it in a big way. It did attract worthwhile crowds. The situation was that you couldn't put it on every week at Mallory and so we ran it about four times a year with a great show. The suspension of the cars was set up for an oval. On other circuits it was like ordinary club racing. It ran for about four years but deteriorated, which was disappointing to us because we were very happy with it.

'As for truck racing – it had taken off. The organisers approached us and said, "What about running at Mallory?" We said that we would give it a go but I felt that with the construction background that I came from there was a risk that big heavy trucks racing around wouldn't do the circuit any good. It was promoted by the Truck Racing Association and involved Andy Marriott with Chris Lowe. When we finally saw the entry we noted that Steve Parrish was

Eurocars in front of race control.

Eurocars at the lake.

Truck racing.

there and he and several other top names had experience of this at home and abroad. Then the MSA track inspector came up and stated, "It's a short circuit and it is very worrying." So he wanted certain spectator areas as no-go areas in case anything flew off. We had to minimise the numbers of marshals around the track, especially those on the outside. Then they made us put a chicane in at the entrance to Gerard's and another one as you came out of the oval at the paddock into the Esses. It was a lot of work. The problem was that the trucks had 1,200bhp. Of course, when they approached the chicane and braked they started tearing up chunks of the track. Anyway, they completed the meeting but we told them that we didn't want them again. It proved a one-off. We had a rush because we were committed to opening the circuit again on the Tuesday. So we had to get the staff in over the Sunday night. It cost us about £40,000 to do the job. We had to resurface all of Gerard's and part of the Esses. Eurocars were a contrast to deal with. They were no problem at all. They did have the most spectacular accidents, fortunately without injury.

'The midweek activities have opened up considerably. When we took over there was none of it. In the early 1990s people were forming companies to run track days both for bikes and for cars. The concept was: why do 100mph up the M1 when you could come to Mallory Park and try it in a race-car or even your own car? Everyman started it off at Mallory. Then they came to us and said that they had an idea for running Formula One cars around. These were older versions. That

Everyman cars on track.

Tyrrell F1.

was very successful on track. Eventually we couldn't cope with the demand of people wanting to hire the track in midweek, which was good news. With practice for the bikes and cars the circuit was in use for the maximum number of dates.

'As a family we were ever so busy. It was a full-time job, as I indicated. In 2001 I became seriously ill and I spent a month in hospital. I had been in intensive care and couldn't go to Mallory Park for about six months. I was laid up at home most of the time. Edwina stayed and looked after me. David had to take over and practically lived at the track. Afterwards, once I was back at Mallory Park, I was now approaching eighty and conscious of the problems that age brings. So we left a lot of responsibility to David and we came over two or three days a week.

'Edwina had suffered respiratory problems all of her life but just kept going. She never smoked and was a teetotaller, which, being involved in motor sport, was quite an achievement. So we eased out of it a bit and David took control.

'Before Edwina passed away in 2003 at the age of seventy-five she was at that meeting in October, presenting the prizes but really struggling. She was on oxygen. She insisted on being there and being out front.

'We had enjoyed an active old age together. Most folk would have wound down but we were running a motor racing circuit! We had always had approaches and some of the people who told us that we were mad to take it on after a few beers were coming to us and asking if they could come in with us. Edwina would never contemplate it.

'Anyway, we had further approaches after she passed away. At first we resisted them. Then I said to David that in view of my health that I thought it was time. David said that without me and his mum he would have to get in new people, so

Dennis Carter.

he had to make a decision. I told him that it was up to him. He replied that he wouldn't do anything without consulting me, which I knew. We had several offers and while most of them wanted to keep motor sport, they wanted to put on all sorts of activities like theme parks. Others wanted to put buildings on. Of course, when we took over there was outline planning permission for houses. In fact, the footings were in place at one time – all ready to start. We never proceeded with it.

'When Dennis Carter of BARC came along, we were good friends. He gelled well with Edwina when they worked together at certain meetings. He had often said to us, "If ever you are thinking of someone to come in with you or doing anything with the circuit, let me know." We approached him and we offered it to him and we also offered it to Everyman because their business had been at Mallory for so long. Some interested bidders may have thrown Everyman out. In view of our friendship with John Farnham, which had gone back fifteen years, we thought that shouldn't happen so we also discussed the opportunity with him. John said that he wanted us to pursue a situation that would ensure a deal to stay there. So David rang Dennis up and he said that he would pop up to see us. We had a good chat. Dennis went away and eventually came back and we shook hands on a deal. We knew Dennis as the operator of Thruxton and other circuits. We wanted the circuit to carry on as Edwina would have wished it. If she had been alive and we had jointly wanted to retire, the only people whom Edwina would have considered selling to was the BARC, purely through Dennis Carter. We knew that he would keep it going as we wanted to and he has. There will, of course, be alterations but it is carrying on as a good club car circuit, a good club bike circuit plus two or three big meetings for the bikes.

John Ward.

'David rang me up from their solicitors − he had gone down with our solicitor to sign up. He said, "Dad, we are just in the meeting now − so if you say no then I'll come back." I replied, "We've agreed it with Dennis so you go ahead." Anyway, he rang me about a half-hour later and told me, "It's all done − and there was no thunderbolt coming down from heaven − so I think that we are alright!"

'I've never had second thoughts about it and I'm sure that David hasn't. I do go but I miss it terribly. BARC kept all the staff so I go to see them regularly. I go to see Wayne and Helen Lovell − they have been there a while. Wayne is a real hands-on foreman whilst Helen was David's "right-hand man" and looks after the administration.

'We were promised that with respect to the staff nothing would alter and they would be left to get on with it. When it came to the appointment of John Ward as the circuit manager, we had known him for years through his involvement with the bike scene for the BRSCC − he was their competitions secretary. So you have a guy there who is well-versed in motor sport. We were very happy to hear of John's installation.

'Finally, I would also like to offer this assessment of Chris Meek. There were lots of guys who were going to do this, that and the other but he's the one who bought

Chris Meek, a winner on and off the track in 1983.

Mallory Park. He said that he would and he did. The first 750 car meeting down there, he came and raced in it. He won it and they didn't let him win it because he owned it! Chris was a great driver. I think that if he hadn't been involved in his property empire that he would have reached Formula One. He was that good. When he used to race and Edwina was competitions secretary, Chris would be winning lots of races, whether it was single-seaters or sports cars or saloons.

'Chris is also a colourful personality. He drives Ferraris and a Rolls-Royce. We often went out with him and he was most entertaining, talking about racing and various other activities that he had taken part in. We did have a couple of run-ins with him over the lease as we could never get a long one. But to Chris business is business – although Edwina got far less wound up with him than I did.

'When he was racing and we were involved with the BRSCC, we would help the BRSCC at their other events at other tracks, with myself as a steward. I will always remember that we went to Snetterton and Chris Meek was racing. Anyway, there was a protest about his car. They said that it wasn't homologated, which means in production car racing that the cars have got to be made by a manufacturer. This was an issue over a Lotus Elan. So we had a meeting of stewards. He hadn't got proof as he hadn't got the papers with him. So we excluded him from the meeting.

Above left: Colin Chapman's statue.

Above right: John Surtees' statue.

Driving back from Norfolk without being spoken to by my wife was quite an experience! Eventually Edwina uttered, "Fancy throwing Chris out!" Then she went on and on! Funnily enough, Chris appealed the decision and produced the information. He did have a tie-up with Colin Chapman and Lotus so it was bound to have been above board. There is now a statue of Colin Chapman at Mallory Park. Chris was friendly with Colin Chapman as well as racing cars for him.

'With John Surtees' statue – a World Champion on both two and four wheels – his own history is so tied in with that of the circuit. He won the first Race of the Year that Clive put on and the last Formula One race there.

'Mike Hailwood won a lot of races at Mallory Park on both two and four wheels. He came back from Formula One to take a big win on a motorcycle at the Isle of Man.

'Roger Clark was local. He lived in Peckleton just down the road. He did race at Mallory in the Tour of Britain – a rally race series. This involved rally stages and race tracks. He also raced in the Eurocars. I asked him, "What do you think of it?" Roger replied, "I've been in some queer rallying situations but coming out of Gerard's the wrong way round is something else!"

Above left: Roger Clark with Edwina Overend.

Above right: Jim Clark's statue.

'Jim Clark obviously raced at the track with great success before his becoming World Formula One Champion.

'Chris commissioned these statues. The set-up was that we did everything at the track including the buildings. Outside of the track was where Chris put the statues.

'The last deal with Chris was for a fifteen-year lease and we had only managed to extract ones for five years before that. This meant that we couldn't raise the money to do anything. The deal with the fifteen-year lease was that we built the new race control and the Hailwood Suite. It was finished in 2004.

'Edwina and David built the circuit up into a good, profitable business. However, the commercial bottom line was not always the influence over decisions. If they could put on good meetings, even as 'loss leaders', they would be put on because they were good for motor sport. That's the way we ran it. We ran it as a friendly business – The Friendly Circuit. This is continuing as far as I can see.'

What of the perspective of others, such as long-serving Don Truman, on the leading players on and off track?

'Edwina Overend was BRSCC competitions secretary and Ron was on the committee. That allowed them to keep some events ticking over at Mallory Park in 1983 while its future was being sorted. Harry Wheatcroft was hovering in the background. He wasn't certain whether he was going to build houses on it or not. While all this was going on I was still clerk of the course for the BRSCC meetings. Chris Meek became the saviour and he is a motor sport enthusiast too. If you talk motor racing with him you can talk for as long as you like, but if you talk business then he is understandably more difficult to deal with.

'Under the Overends Mallory Park became "The Friendly Circuit". Edwina Overend was a larger-than-life character. As for doing business with Edwina – if she liked you she would do business with you. If she didn't like you and even if you had the finest deal in creation she wouldn't do business with you. Edwina did all her dealings with the heart and not the head.

'Edwina had the most astonishing memory. Somebody would come along who hadn't been to Mallory for ten years – she knew his name, his wife's name, the name of the kids. It was quite astonishing. She would invite all the bigwigs to the circuit for hospitality but make most of the sandwiches herself. She wasn't proud and was great at public relations.

'I did have one or two little ding-dongs with her. There was one particular year when the meetings had been so designed that there was very little spare time. There is a 6 p.m. curfew. I would get a phone call from Edwina once it

Jonathan Palmer.

Martin Brundle, Formula Ford 200, 1980.

Nigel Mansell.

Ayrton Senna.

went past six: "Don't you know what time it is?" I did but only then would I ask for the chequered flag to be put down.

'I used to take Ron down to the main board meetings in London, for I was chairman of the BRSCC for ten years. I like David. He is a good accountant. I wondered about some of his ideas, however. Ron was a director of a building company in Walsall but turned it in eventually to assist Edwina. To run a circuit takes a fair amount of time and commitment.

'They couldn't do anything major to the circuit for the bulk of their management because Chris Meek wouldn't grant them a long enough lease. If you've only got a five-year lease you are not going to spend half a million quid are you?

Martin Brundle.

'There became a shift to the bikes because that was where the money was. They attracted bigger gates. I have no interest in motorbikes and my memories of cars also involves seeing drivers like Ayrton Senna, Jonathan Palmer and Martin Brundle coming through. Jonathan Palmer was a bloody good driver, of international standard. I thought that Senna would make it to the very top, as I did Jackie Stewart in a previous era at Mallory. Graham Hill was what I describe as a "B-class brilliant driver". He had to work hard at it. He was good but he wasn't instinctive. Nigel Mansell was brilliant and he had sphericals two feet across the dashboard. He is also a good lad. In later years I saw him being followed to race control at Donington by thousands of kids. He had a big overcoat on, a poacher's

Nigel Mansell.

overcoat with pockets everywhere. Every time a fresh kid appeared he would put his hand in his pocket and fetch out a signed photograph for them. The problem with Nigel is that if you stick a mike in front of him he becomes a whinge-pot. If you are talking to him he is absolutely marvellous.

'Looking at the end of my long period at Mallory, it was enjoyable. As far as I am concerned I think that a really good club meeting is better racing than anything that is going. The trouble is that the club meetings don't bring the gate. You have got to have a recognisable name or people don't come in.

'When people ask me about my favourite memory over the long stretch that I had at Mallory – well, there used to be a sales manager called Stuart. Apparently he invited a bloke to come and visit the circuit. He came to Mallory in a two-seater microlight, landed it at Gerard's and parked on the grass. This was about

Don Truman.

ten to nine. I had practice to start at 9 a.m. – times used to depend on dialogue with the local church. I came steaming around and this gentlemen told me that he had been invited. I asked, "Who invited you?" He replied, "David, I think." So I got on the radio to David Overend, who told me that he knew nothing about it. So I told this bloke to sod off a bit quickly. I came back in race control and stated, "That's not too bad – we only started practice thirty seconds late!"

'Apparently there was a motor sport reporter fairly close by. Anyway, I managed to do the drivers' briefing and one of the comments that I used to bring in was "The black stuff is yours, the green stuff is ours – so keep off it!" The next week in *Motoring News* it said, "There is no truth in the rumour that the Clerk of the Course Don Truman told this man – 'the blue stuff is yours, p—— off!'"

'1999 was the last time that I acted as clerk of the course. The following year I became club steward – so I am still active. I've done all the BARC meetings at Mallory Park. The stewards judge incidents. The MSA steward is chairman and there are two club stewards. If anybody protests a clerk's decision then the hearing is conducted by the stewards. My Mallory Park days are not over – but I do regret that Ron didn't put a lift in race control!'

WHEELS WITHIN WHEELS

With motorcycle racing a constant factor in the success and survival of Mallory Park since 1956 there are many overlapping memories of those from clubman to legend, from historic to contemporary, starting with Arnie Fletcher: 'I first went to Mallory Park as a spectator in the 1950s. You had to queue to get in. At the Race of the Year you stood shoulder to shoulder. From that time onwards I saw the likes of Rex Butcher, Ray Pickrell, Derek Minter, John Cooper, Mike Hailwood and Paul Smart produce a high level of British-based competition.

'I started to ride in the 1960s on an AJS 7R. The first time that I had an outing at Mallory Park I came down with three other riders at the hairpin and landed in a heap. These days the track is safer, especially at Gerard's. Now there is a gravel trap. There used to be a bank that finished the careers of several riders when they went over the fence there.

'I had gone to Mallory with a friend who was entered on a 250 Rudge. I had never done any racing and was a bit nervous. Having applied the front brakes I was thrown over the handlebars. I definitely had the slowest bike on track. At the hairpin I was flat out in top and really didn't need to brake.

'There weren't the club races when I started out, only national races. So having bought myself a bike I couldn't get rides on a regular basis. I used to fill in my entry form and take it around to the local secretary, Jack Walton, who was based in Derby. However, this didn't guarantee an outing at all. Then racing started up on old aerodromes and a "Racing for Sport" category at Oulton Park meant two or three meetings a season.

'I became involved with Keith Heuwen when he phoned me at my motorcycle business at Melton Mowbray. Keith had a TZ 350 and told me that he couldn't

Motorcycles of various vintages.

get it to work. Keith was based at Woolaston. He brought the bike over and we sorted the ignition out. At club level Keith began to win every race that he rode in. Eventually Keith asked us to convert his 350 to a 500. Now we had a 500 three-cyclinder Yamaha that we had built in 1974 for Steve Manship to compete with at Mallory Park and Steve had won his first race out on the bike. So we offered it to Keith rather than carry out a conversion. It was a one-off ride and Keith went out and won it. So we gave him a go on a TZ 750 and he got on well with it.

'When the 1979 season came along he asked if he could ride that bike. We wondered if this was a mistake as we were not sure how Keith would go on it overall. But he was focused and won the British Championship. This opened doors for him. By performance he was chosen for the Transatlantic series, which he was pitched into at Brands, Mallory and Oulton over one weekend. At Mallory Park in particular he was very competitive and he repeated that standard at the circuit in 1980 too.

'Since then I've remained active at Mallory Park as a rider of the 250 and 350 Yamahas, taking part in support races at Mallory Park during Classic meetings up to 2004.

'Mallory is really challenging as it is effectively five corners: Gerard's, the Esses, the Hairpin, the Bus Stop and the Devil's Elbow. You cannot afford to be bad at any of them. You gulp going in and at the Devil's Elbow if you fall you will hit something. You can't be slow on the straight as it is crucial to the impetus of your race. You have really got to get a good run to hold a position at Gerard's, while the Bus Stop and Edwina's are narrow. Practically only one rider can pass through so you have to queue. At the hairpin you have to break as late as possible. If you are too quick at the Bus Stop you will fall off. It is a very challenging circuit to ride, whatever your level, but it can be very satisfying too.'

Next, some more insight from John Cooper: 'I rode at Mallory in 1956, at the time that I was in the Army, on a Royal Enfield. Being in the Army I didn't get another ride until 1958. I rode a BSA Gold Star and an Alf Briggs JAP. Then I built a Triumph Cub in 1959 with a James frame and a Triumph engine. I rode that there. Then a chap called Russ Warren took a bit of a fancy to my riding style. He had a rider from Derby whom he was supporting give up and I got the ride on a Panda Gold Star then. I had a 350 and a 500 Gold Star followed by a 350 Norton that I rode there in 1961. Mallory became a local venue to go and earn a few quid on a Sunday afternoon. Mallory Park was the place to go for motorcycling in the East Midlands. There was no M1 originally, so it was nice for people from Leicester, Derby and Nottingham to go to. It wasn't too far.

'Unfortunately between 1961 and 1965 I worked for my Dad in a clothing shop, which I absolutely hated. He wouldn't give me any time off to go motorcycle racing at all. I used to just ride on a Sunday. I wasn't allowed to have Saturdays off. In general, people couldn't afford to go practising in those days. Riders now don't expect to have to go to work, because they think that motorbike racing is a career. They don't work in the week as they also get sponsors. When I was riding you had to stand on your own two feet. It was hard.

'As a youngster I took part in trials and a bit of scrambling. I wasn't very good at it as I wore spectacles. I was about seven stone and I was very small. I suffered a lot of wheelspin and I wasn't very good at it because of my size. When I went to watch road racing at Alton Towers I used to think that it looked easier than trials and scrambles. The first time that I ever rode at Osmaston – a stately home with a little three-quarter-mile track around it – I felt that I could go on from there. By the time that I had got back from watching the Isle of Man TT I had received my call-up papers. So I did two years national service in the catering corps from July 1956 to June 1958.

'There wasn't an opportunity to be a full-time racer. In fact I've never been a full-time racer by definition. I have always worked and raced. I think that has stood me in good stead now because I have four industrial units and four houses that I rent out. So when I decide to retire I will have enough money. A lot of

Jim Redman.

the lads in the early days like Bill Ivy, Mike Hailwood and Jim Redman used to live on the continent when racing. Five-star hotels and running Ferraris or Maseratis meant that they were spending a lot of money, whereas I was working and saving up money.

'In the 1960s my big rival at Mallory Park was Derek Minter – and at other circuits too, especially Brands Hatch. You didn't have the motorway system. It used to take seven hours to reach Brands Hatch. It was a long way. You used to have to leave overnight and sleep in the back of the van.

'With Mallory Park I did go there a lot. I was a bit fortunate in many respects because I used to do the testing for Dunlop tyres. They made the triangular tyres and it suited Mallory down to the ground because it was a long, long bend around Gerard's. The Esses were quite a long turn too. The Dunlop tyres really suited it. Others, like Derek Minter, used Avon tyres. Then, when Avon packed up, I was used to the triangular tyres and my rivals were struggling with them. So they tried to use the old Avon tyres. They didn't like the way the bikes turned into the corners like Gerard's and the Esses. It was a bit of a break for me. When Bob McIntyre was sadly killed I took the testing of Dunlop tyres over, meeting by meeting. They used to stick the super rubber in when everybody else had ordinary rubber, like they do these days. Sometimes they put better rubber on for one of the top stars.

'I remember when I won the big race at Mallory in 1970. Paul Butler, who is now the race director for the Moto GP, made me a tyre with all the same markings as everybody else's but it was a soft rubber. I sort of ran away with it on a 350 with other riders on 500s and 750s. I had been the first motorcyclist to ride at Oulton Park in 1966 with slick tyres. Dunlop said to me, "Can you test these tyres? Don't look at them and tell me what you think."

'Derek Minter wasn't very tall and he never made a very good start. He could catch up about three-quarters of a straight at Mallory. Ray Petty, who worked on his bikes, was a bit of a smartie. I thought, "How does Derek Minter manage to catch me up?" I knew that I was going as hard as I could. I was riding on the 350 and 500 Nortons. I had a friend who bought the bikes and we would split the prize money. I would pay my own expenses. People didn't dish out money like they do today. In British Superbikes they want a million pounds to start a season. It's a damn lot of money. When I was riding I was earning £500 a week and that was a lot to me.

'Arthur Taylor, the clerk of the course at Mallory Park, was an awkward old bugger. Many regarded him as a nasty man but I did get on good terms with him when he became an old man. He was on his own after his wife died and I used to go around and see that he was fed properly. Much to my surprise he left me £45,000 in his will! A fortnight later Russ Warren, who used to enter me in races, died and left me £65,000. I suddenly ended up with £100,000 and put that towards my business.

'A lot of people associated with the earlier days of Mallory Park would recognise Arthur Taylor as being an awkward old man. I would take him a bottle of scotch because he liked a drink and I believed that he had no money. He had been a solicitor's clerk in Derby. It would be fair to say that he didn't have many friends but I befriended him because I felt sorry for him really. It wasn't always sweetness and light. In 1967 I broke a collarbone at Aberdare Park in South Wales. My return back to racing was at Mallory Park. I had my collarbone strapped up. Jack Walton, who was the secretary at Mallory for the East Midlands ACU, gave me permission to have a pusher off the back of the grid. When I stood on the back of the grid with that pusher, Arthur Taylor came along and stated, "You can't have a pusher because you haven't asked me!" I told him that I had asked the secretary of the meeting and he said that I could. Arthur Taylor insisted that I couldn't. So I had to stand on the front of the grid at my position. I had a bad start and as I got around Devil's Elbow on the first lap, Bill Ivy had a coming-together with somebody, fell off and his bike was lying across the track. I hit his bike, went over the top and broke my other collarbone. Now I had two broken collarbones! The first bloke walking towards me was Arthur Taylor and in my pain I uttered, "You bloody awful bastard – if it wasn't for you, I wouldn't

John Cooper,
Race of the Year
1965.

have ended up like this!" I didn't speak to him for about two years. I was walking through Derby one day and I saw him walking towards me and I exclaimed, "About time that we said hello isn't it?"

'After the highlights of the subsequent years – not just with my Race of the Year victories at Mallory Park but being British Champion and *MCN* Man of the Year on three occasions – my racing came to an end in 1973. That year I was planning to do the TT but I fell off at Brands Hatch and broke a leg. It was a compound fracture and it hurt so badly. When Robin Miller, a reporter, and his wife came to see me in hospital I told them that they would never see me race a motorcycle again. I was in so much pain and I was into my thirties. That was on 28 May 1973.

Barry Briggs.

'I have good memories, however, of my career. What I like about motorbike racing is that there are no staff problems. Get a pair of handlebars and a pair of footrests. Put your feet on the footrest, your hands on the handlebars and you ride around with no bugger telling you what to do. You do it your way. That's what I like about racing. You are on your own. Suck it and see.

'I've had lots of good little races at Mallory – it's been really good. When I built my 350 Yamsel – it was a Yamaha in a Seeley frame. I went to Mallory Park in 1969 and I rode a 350 RJS and it was very slow but it was a really lovely machine. I also had a 350 Yamaha that multi-World Speedway Champion Barry Briggs had brought me back from America and that I bought from him. The Yamaha went like stink but it wouldn't steer. The Yamaha pitched me off and I broke some fingers and hurt my ribs. Charlie Wilkinson, who owned Cadwell Park, was standing at this corner and I landed at his feet. It scared him so much that he paid me some start money when I got back! He was concerned because I had fallen off and hurt myself. I was lying in bed that night and thought, "If I put the engine out of the Yamaha in the Seeley frame I would have a bloody good bike!" I thought that I would call it a Yamsel. I built this bike and it was unbelievable. I eventually broke every lap record and won race after race. The first time that I rode it was at Mallory Park in 1969. Tony Rutter, Michael's dad, beat me. I had a high top gear. I should have geared it and used four gears instead of five. Putting it in top gear killed it. He just beat me and I thought, "You won't do that twice, mate." I then put a proper gearbox in it, got on and won. I won forty races outright. It was a marvellous bike. A good Mallory link again in my life. That was a good home base.

'When I built my Yamsel, I finished it on a Friday lunchtime and I went out of Derby on a back road with no number-plates or anything on it. I went out and back in no time at all. I thought, "This is going to be good." It was good. Colin Seeley went on to produce them for me and I sold them all over the world.

'I keep my links with Mallory Park. I've been given passes over the years and I sometimes go and stand on the outside to watch. I go to the Post-TT every year. It's really nice. Edwina Overend was marvellous. It was a great pity when she died. The last time that I saw her I took her some fine Crown Derby but she didn't look well at all. You would go there and enjoy cups of tea and legs of chicken. It was a social occasion. I used to take my pals from the Red Arrows. In fact I still get requests to go to Mallory Park. I've ridden at the Post-TT and have been offered expenses. I've asked for a half-dozen tickets to give to my friends rather than have the money. We go and have a good day out.'

The generations gradually move forward with Paul Smart: 'I spent my teenage years in a transport café that my parents ran. We lived in sight and sound of

A Yamsel, 1970.

John Cooper with Edwina Overend.

Brands Hatch. Then we moved near to Maidstone running a café where the motorcyclists used to collect at night. From the age of twelve this gave me my appetite for motorcycles. We are talking the late 1950s when the motorbike was a popular form of transport, BSAs and Triumphs – British bikes. As I said this whetted my appetite for motorcycles but then again we had no money.

'I left school at the first possible opportunity and became an apprentice boatbuilder. In 1958 I start riding my first bike, which was quite a large one at 350cc. It probably went as quick as a modern 50. The transition from riding a bike for leisure and as a form of transport to riding in competition came about as I had a big group of friends who rode motorcycles. Lots of my buddies were really enthusiastic about racing but had no chance. Lots of them were GPO telegram riders. We were all enthusiastic about racing, bearing in mind that this was an era when grass-track was strong in Kent and Brands Hatch was just up the road.

'We started visiting circuits and we went to Mallory Park. That was quite an event before motorways. It was quite a distance, the same with Snetterton. Obviously in those days we went to spectate for we just loved our motorcycles.

'In my youth there was therefore absolutely no chance of going racing. I was twenty-two before I raced. A lot of my buddies did manage to go riding

Mike Hailwood.

grass-track on home-brewed "bangers" basically. Then the Charles Mortimor Racing School started with Grieves 250s in 1963 based at Shere in Surrey. He had an old Thames van with a horsebox at the back with a dozen bikes. He toured British circuits. He had a day at Brands and I think it was £15. You could go for twenty laps. I went there and thought that it was wonderful. I had actually done a couple of high-speed trials at Silverstone on a BSA twin Triumph. I also had a go at sidecar grass-track racing – it was cheaper to split the cost.

'My first race bike was the 125 Bultaco, which I bought off a local guy at Paddock Wood. In my first year I rode in three races – that is all you could afford. Having bought my first race bike I realised it was time to get a driving licence too! I didn't even own a car or a van. All my buddies clubbed together and bought me a van. I had to work out how to get it home.

'As for my hikes up to Mallory Park to spectate – they would have been for international meetings. At my first visit there I remember getting a book signed by Mike Hailwood. Our local guy was Derek Minter. He was the "King of Brands" but Mike Hailwood was a step above him. Mike Hailwood was a hero. Even though I progressed to know him personally through my racing career I found it difficult to treat him as an equal. He was outstanding. One of my first visits to Mallory was at a Post-TT meeting. It was a big adventure. The TT and then to Mallory Park was the maximum that you could afford as a youngster.

Going abroad was out of the question. Although Mallory Park was a distance, tracks like Oulton Park were at the end of the earth. I remember the M1 being built, of course.

'It never dawned on me that I would have been that good at racing. I didn't have any targets when I set out. My parents would not have had the money to help anyway. I never looked too far ahead because going racing was beyond my wildest dreams. The first bike, a 125 Bultaco, cost £120 and the van cost my pals £20. It was so rusty that when you went round a corner the doors would swing open. However, it was so wonderful to be able to do it. If I had a good race meeting it was fabulous. I never looked at a season because I had no idea where the money was coming from. I always had a job and would take another one in the evening. You had to accumulate enough money to put yourself in the public eye so that you are seen to be doing well. People don't spot talent when you are in twentieth place.

'My first race at Mallory Park was with that Bultaco 125. It was incredibly unreliable. I actually led the race until it seized. To me the fact that I hadn't even finished the race didn't really matter to me. I had gone past everybody in the field from back to front.

'My career took a huge step forward in my second year of racing when I had enough money to buy a 125cc Honda. This I shared with John Button, a pal of mine, and rode alternate meetings. Then I started to perform much better than my friend. I was the faster so John sacrificed his share of the bike. I then had my first couple of wins on the bike.

'As for racing at Mallory Park, the problem I would say is that it was so simple. Basically it is four or five corners. You would find that there were lots of circuit specialists. There is always a challenge to learning. Gerard's was a problem but probably only on 500s in those days. The small bikes would go down one gear going into it. The reality was that the 125 was flat out from Devil's Elbow right through. I hated hairpins. Hairpins were where I fell off. A hairpin only has one line covering the shortest distance. Mallory Park didn't have certain safety features. If your brake failed – which is what practically ended my career – you went straight into the Armco, which was on the edge of the tarmac. This meant that you had zero chance of escaping serious injury. So the Mallory Park hairpin, in my opinion, was an absolute disaster area. However, if you try to make it as safe as possible you turn it into Silverstone, where there is somebody racing in the distance. I'm not sure that you would want to see that. To ride the hairpin was actually very easy. It wasn't skill – you basically had to work your cornering technique according to your motorcycling ability. If you had braking points then you weren't actually that good because unless you can actually calculate it, you are not going to outbrake anyone anyway.

'Gerard's is a 180-degrees bend and the shortest distance is on the inside. The circuit was much nicer before you had the Bus Stop. Thank God that was after my day. I can't think of anything less imaginative than the Bus Stop. It is only surpassed by Edwina's. In my day, when I first went there, Mallory Park was challenging. The racing was always very, very close. From a spectator's point of view it was excellent. You didn't have to be a highly skilled rider to be up the front but it took cunning to win the race. This was because there weren't that many bends to show how much better you could twist on a corner. It's only five corners. The Esses would come up very quickly. The faster the bike meant the Esses became a challenge. I can only talk pre-Bus Stop and pre-Edwina's. The hairpin was just a procession and accidents tend to happen at slow corners with motorbikes. It might be great for cars but all this chicane business for motorbikes is difficult. It breaks collarbones and increases the likelihood of problems. In my opinion Edwina's has even accelerated that problem because it brings everybody into a bunch. It is difficult to believe that anybody who has been involved in the sport would have thought any differently.

'In the old days, before these obstructions, the circuit was pretty good fun, other than the fact that Mallory had a large grass bank to contend with, which could have launched a car or a motorcycle – so I do understand that bit. If you wanted to go racing, you had to go out there and risk life and limb. I look at Mallory Park and think that I would have liked to have sat down with half a dozen people and said, "Look what we could have done that would have been a lot better than Edwina's and the Bus Stop." Perhaps something could still be achieved. You can't lose too much out of the middle so perhaps lose some car parking. Obviously planning issues come into it and with the village in proximity there is possible sensitivity for an extension.

'I did have a lot of success at Mallory despite my start. Unfortunately in 1974 my career was effectively ended there. I hit the Armco because I had a brake failure going into the hairpin on the last lap. Barry Sheene and myself were dicing, in fact we were often at the front. We were first and second anyway. I had taken my front fender off because the engine was getting too hot, so the front fender and the brake get tired. It rubs against the tyre in one or two places. Going into the hairpin is one of the very few spots that you are hard on the brakes. The forks get compressed.

'Up to then I had suffered a couple of pretty big crashes there. I had fallen off at the Esses, never fallen off at Gerard's, but inevitably it was at the hairpin. I usually fell off coming out of the hairpin.

'My first race back after I broke my legs at Mallory – was at Mallory Park! I finished second to Steve Parrish. There was a psychological challenge to a certain extent but it was a mechanical failure that got me. I had total confidence in my

One of the highlights of Paul Smart's career – winning the Imola 200 in 1972.

own riding ability. The problem when you are out for the best part of a year is that you lose your job. People don't employ the services of someone with two legs broken. So it was kind of stepping backwards for four years. I was married and we had a son. I wasn't prepared to go through the whole rigmarole again. I probably made a hasty decision – I could have got another three or four years profitable riding out of it if I had just got my head straight. In reality I had a lot of good races at Mallory Park because it was always tight racing. Like any short circuit – particularly with a hairpin, which is a one-line corner – you had to make a good start. That was absolutely essential in the days when you had bump starts. It led to more tension on the grid and you had to have a motorcycle that did start. From the back it was very hard to get through the field of riders bunched up at the hairpin.

'The grids at Mallory were in excess of thirty-five – that's a busy circuit. You were lapping very quickly. One of the reactions that I found was that you were pleased to graduate into national racing because everybody on the grid was more experienced and more consistent.

'In the modern era I now have a son, Scott, racing but we didn't have the same enthusiasm that Maggie's dad, Frank Sheene, had for Barry. Of course, we had seen the downside. We knew that only one guy in a thousand makes

Scott Smart in action.

it. It is bloody hard to make the grade. You can also hurt yourself really badly. So we didn't push too hard. Perhaps we should have done – and when he was younger.

'Barry was a very intelligent person and I think that Scott has a lot of his natural ability and intelligence. Academically Scott is good and was studying for a Masters degree in Physics. This is possibly to his detriment as a racer because he is always trying to have perfection with his machinery. He will get around that because everyone has to ride around their problems. Scott has been superb around Mallory – better than me. His racing in 2004 at Mallory Park saw the best racing day of his career. It was beset with stoppages because unfortunately that is the problem. They stopped the race three times. So basically he ran four races there that day. You have to start on the same grid positions and you have to go right through again to get in front. He won the British Superbikes Championship and he was outstanding.'

Someone who has had an influence on Scott Smart but whose career as a rider and as a constructor covers many personalities over several decades is Colin Seeley: 'My father always had motorbikes. We were into Vincents in the days that I remember as a young man. We used to go to Dartford Heath on a Sunday

Sidecar racing of the era.

and had the opportunity of learning to ride the Vincent sidecar. I was fourteen. In those days I used to cycle out to Brands Hatch – 1950 – when it was first a tarmac track. My hero then was George Brown, who worked for Vincents, and Ted Davies, who was a works tester but raced sidecars. I used to hang over the fence thinking, "I wouldn't mind having a go at that."

I started my own motorcycle business in 1954. I was eighteen years of age. I've been in business since. So I was a retailer/repairer for about eleven years. I was taking part in scrambles, grass-track, hill climbing and sprints around Kent from 1954 to 1960. Then I went sidecar road racing when I had some money.

'The first outfit that I bought was an ex-Eric Oliver. He was an ex-World Champion in his day on the Nortons. I bought his Manx Norton, which we rode at Snetterton. My first race was in 1960. The machine was a load of rubbish to be honest. So I thought that I had to do better than this. At that time I was an agent for Matchless motorcycles down at Plumstead. We bought a brand new Matchless G50. I used to sell sidecars in those days. Canterbury Sidecars made a racing sidecar. So I had bought one too. I cut it all around, welded some fittings on and bolted them so that we had a Matchless racing side-car outfit. From the start of the 1961 season to the entry for the TT in 1961 – remembering that it was our first proper year of sidecar racing – we got a restricted international racing licence.

'I first rode at Mallory Park in 1961. It wasn't really our favourite circuit because you had no time to think. It was all go. Brands Hatch short circuit was very much like that as well but a little more forgiving. You had the main straight. You had the bottom straight. But Mallory Park was certainly one circuit that you couldn't muck about at. You had to get cracking.

'Gerard's is not flat out in any particular gear but it was quite challenging. I had some good rides there. It's difficult when you look back sometimes because you are so much younger and you are full of enthusiasm. You just take it in your stride. If I was doing it now I would be thinking, "Bloody hell! What am I doing here?" It was a bit hairy and physically it was quite tough as well, particularly around Gerard's. You are holding a sidecar outfit. I used to have big strong arms in those days – you needed them to hold on, particularly with the old outfits. It is a bend that just goes around and around and around. They are talking of changing it and putting a chicane in. It has been approved by some of the Superbike teams but it is getting too quick now. That is one of the problems. You really have to throw it in there and keep it going. Go round and round – almost like it was a straight.

'I only did two club meetings in my life and went straight into nationals. After national I progressed to international level and reached Grand Prix level. I had started out just wanting to have a go and never dreamt that I would end up competing for the World Championship.

'When I was running my business I was sponsoring a lad called Sid Missen from the Isle of Man. We decided to improve the Matchless bike. So I decided to make a frame. Why did I get into that? Well, the title of my forthcoming book provides the clue: "Seemed a Good Idea at the Time."

'John Cooper had the most original Seeley that is in existence. It won so many races. Derek Minter rode it to begin with, then John Blanchard and finally John Cooper. John bought it eventually. From that time onwards we just moved on. I now employ twenty-seven people full time. Setting up a business like that took a fair amount of investment. I was still racing to earn money in 1966. That year at Mallory Park, Fritz Scheidegger got killed there right in front of me at the hairpin. A lovely guy, Fritz, and a brilliant rider who had good bikes. It was an unlimited race and a guy called Brown was leading it. I was second. We came through the back straight, through the Esses and Fritz came alongside of me. I knew instantly that he wasn't going to stop. I just knew because I wasn't going slow into the hairpin. He didn't stop. He suffered a failure of the rear brake. They went straight on. Fritz was catapulted over the Armco. John Robinson, the passenger, broke both legs. Medical aid couldn't get to Fritz in time. That was really sad. The next day I had to race at Oulton Park. I won both races there from Pip Harris and took home £400. I bought a milling machine with that. So then I gradually built the equipment up. I would stress that we didn't assemble machines – we made them. We ran our own race team and we won the 500cc championship in 1968 and 1969 with Dave Croxford.

'We did the first bikes for Ducati. We did twenty-four different models altogether. We did the Seeley Hondas. We did the Phil Read replicas for Honda UK. The G50 Mark Four model is entirely Seeley. The engine was the original Matchless design but we manufactured it all at Belvedere. We did test at Mallory Park and we also had lots of fantastic results at the circuit with Dave Croxford. He used to have 'The Master of Mallory' as a title. He won that in 1968. Mallory Park played quite an important part in the whole scheme of things. Success there promoted the name. We made an impact pretty quickly and everyone heard of us.

'The Yamsel was a Seeley-framed Yamaha, which John Cooper conceived. We built a lightweight 350 for him. He was a big Seeley fan anyway and we have remained good friends. It was so successful that we got into producing them. Our bikes were sold all over the world. John was a professional racer but he

Sidecar racers of the modern era – Steve Webster and Tony Hewitt.

also had business premises so we agreed that he was able to sell them as well. My contact with the top racers was through my own sidecar racing and success. Generally speaking, the sidecar fraternity kept themselves to themselves. I was one of the rare guys who always got involved with the solo riders because I was a sponsor too. I also had a reputation for my outfits being immaculate. I think that the solo riders appreciated that. Lots of sidecar guys were already regarded as chucking oil down on the circuit. The solo riders were falling off on it and were none too pleased but I had the good reputation. I knew all the riders through my own involvement with the Grand Prix. It all really went from there. So when I started to build the solos, there wasn't any difficulty.

'I knew Stan and Mike Hailwood – Stan through his ownership of "Kings of Oxford". Mike used to write a column and he gave me a mention – this was in the very early days of the business. He had liked what he had seen. Then he wanted a bike for Oulton Park for the Gold Cup. This was in 1968. He had already been on to me about riding at Brands. He liked what we were doing. He liked my approach. I think that he wanted to do us a favour. Everybody wanted him to ride their bikes, as you can imagine. He chose to ride mine on that occasion. He won the Oulton Gold Cup in 1968, beating John Cooper. Phil Read was third. That in itself was a great story but Mike won an Omega watch and he gave it to me. This is obviously greatly treasured. Then in 1969 he was invited to Mallory Park but he didn't have any works bikes at his disposal. So he rang me up and asked if I could help out with a bike, which I promptly did. He won the 500 race and finished fifth in the Race of the Year. However, he was the quickest single-cylinder rider out there as always. I remember Duckhams sponsored the meeting and that Mike was very nervous on the day. Dickie Davies from ITV was there to present live for the television coverage. One of the pictures that I have of him is our standing at the start and my appearing to say: "Mike, this is the way to do it!"

'In the modern era I ran several teams in the mid-1990s including the official Castrol Honda team. After that I got involved with a rider called Karl Muggeridge, who went on to win the World Supersport Championship. We used to go to Mallory Park testing. The first actual test was there. Stuart Hicken of Hawk Kawasaki is no longer based at Mallory but he stated, "I don't rate that lad." He became World Champion in 2004. Eventually Karl had moved on and I thought that I would ease right off – especially with all the travelling around the country.

'Then Paul Smart came and asked if he and Scott could see me. We sat down in my office and Paul asked my advice on Scott's career. I remember saying, "If you want my help then first we have to get people to like you." For Scott could be a bit lairy. I also told him, "You need to listen." He said that he would do that and I've been helping him. Everybody that I've introduced him to since has commented what a good lad he is. He is a nice lad but the trouble is that he is so intelligent compared, with all due respect, to half of the field – they can resent him. Anyway, he did settle down and I did get him into the Hawk team in 2003, based at Mallory Park. He had a good year in 2004. The highlight was an absolutely brilliant ride to beat all the top dogs around Mallory Park for the British Superbikes title. I was involved in 2005 in all the negotiations of his going to the Rizla Suzuki team. Then it all went wrong for him, which was a combination of the bikes, the team and himself because you just lose it when matters are not right.

'For a rider, Scott's Uncle Barry was mechanically knowledgeable because of Frank Sheene. Scott is very good like that as well. Smart by name and Smart by nature. Scott's powers of analysis are against him sometimes on the track, however. I tell him to just get out there and bloody well ride, which is what Mike Hailwood used to do. Get out and go and race.

'If you say that Mallory was dangerous in the past, so were many of the circuits. Matters have improved. On the hairpin they have put that chicane in to reduce the speeds going around the Elbow. That wanted doing differently in

Karl Muggeridge.

my book. It was done there to reduce the speeds because the bikes were getting too quick. At the Elbow they didn't have the run-off areas. Now they have got a decent run-off area. In the earlier days riders got hurt there – of that there is no question. There was nowhere to go, you see. Now that they have done the pit area and everything else it has all been moved back a bit, which has improved it. They put Edwina's around the back and what this has done is slow them down but increased the speed going up to the hairpin. Now they are going to put this chicane in at Gerard's and I said to John Ward, "What's the score? Is it going to be a flying corner?"

'I've known the Mallory Park manager, John Ward, since he was a little boy. His father, John Ward Senior, was a travelling marshal at Brands Hatch. With John Ward Senior, I was on the race committee of the Greenwich District Motorcycle Club that were part of the combine that ran Brands meetings in those days. So I have known the family a long time. When John Ward was the clerk of the course at our meetings and others at Brands I ran the Rotary Nortons in 1994 to win the championship, and we were actually sponsored by Brands Hatch for our national campaign.

'John Ward and I go back a long way and I have always worked well with him. John is a no-nonsense guy – he does dig his feet in sometimes. John is also good on the cars as he worked with the BRSCC and when he left Brands Hatch he worked on a car series with a company based there.

'I knew the Overends very well and was involved with two major events at Mallory Park. One was the Seeley Day in 1999 and the other was a Norton day, when John Surtees came along as a guest. The Seeley Day was David Overend's idea, to be honest. He said that he would like to have a Seeley Day at a Post-TT event and came out with the words "while you are still with us, rather than when you are gone!"

'We had a great weekend. We had about 100 Seeleys with loads of top riders. They booked us into the same hotel the night before so everybody was having a good evening on the Saturday night. On the Sunday night Mallory organised a dinner with Steve Hislop there. We had a few speeches and a very nice evening. We also had some presentations. So the Seeley Day was very successful. For the fiftieth anniversary I've got Bonhams to sponsor it. Mortons Press, which publishes all the major magazines like *Classic Racer* and *Classic Motorcycle*, are going to provide the coverage. John is going along with a two-day event for that weekend, which is what I wanted in the first place. I know a lot of people in the sport and that can be useful for making further introductions.

'My happy memories of Mallory Park are of my own results there, the results that we had with Seeley, which were awesome, and in more recent years success with Scott Smart.'

Colin Seeley talks with Mike Hailwood before the Race of the Year on 21 September 1969.
(Picture by B.R. Nicholls, courtesy of Mortons Media Group)

Which brings us to the perspective of the young man himself: 'Having Paul Smart as a father meant that I rode bikes from very young. However, it was always competitive around Dad – even going around a field. He was competitive about everything that he did and I inherited this – even impacting on my academic pursuits. I studied Physics at the Imperial College of Science. Even there I wanted to be top of the class but my sporting instincts increasingly came into play. Originally I had no intention to be a road racer and much preferred motocross. With great reluctance my parents said that they would support my foray into the territory so well occupied by my father and by my uncle, Barry Sheene. They anticipated that I wouldn't do that well in my 400cc event but in my first race I came third. This latent talent eventually led to a conflict between university studies and my racing ambition. It was also the basis of some conflict with my parents, but that is not unusual in a sporting context. Dad was supportive in the sense that he came along originally as a mechanic but that side of it is not really his scene. So I began to build up my own support team.

'I concentrated on the 250cc scene with an aim of reaching the Grand Prix. I was on a Honda RS 250 and did well from the off at British and European level, eventually winning the British 250 Championship in my third season. By a quirk I ended up in the 500 Grand Prix after that.

'I have positive memories of Mallory Park – particularly having won both the 250cc and 500cc there in 1996. I'm not a great fan of the circuit overall but always seem to perform well at the Esses, which surprised me. I'm glad that they improved Gerard's with a run-off area. Although Gerard's goes on forever, at least there are a variety of lines. I'm quite adept at the hairpin as I've always been good at braking. I can hold my line and I'm strong on left-hand bends too. So Edwina's has been a plus for me in recent years.

'I won the British Superbikes at Mallory Park in 2004 after a most frustrating race that had been held up under the pace car every time I led well. I had to keep forcing myself out front. When it came to the final dash to the flag the others in pursuit would have ended up crashing if they had tried to take me. I just went for it. It was a great relief after all that frustration.

'I was particularly pleased for Stuart Hicken who was running my team – Hawk Kawasaki – out of Mallory Park. A home victory for Stuart was very satisfying. Stuart had some very good mechanics who worked very hard and I always believe in seeking development. As we were a comparatively small team I had to muck in and help. I enjoyed that and it helps to teach you to look after yourself.'

One person who knows how to look after himself, both as an ex-rider and current team manager, is Rob McElnea: 'My first memories of Mallory are very

Scott Smart.

much as a spectator. I used to come along with my father, I was one of those annoying kids in the paddock.

'I have to say that it wasn't one of our favourites – it's quite a specialist sort of track. We lived in Lincolnshire and went to Cadwell Park. Mallory Park was always a tough one to come to because it was such a unique type of circuit with Gerard's and the Devil's Elbow. You did get a lot of specialists here and so it was always tough to get a result.

'My Dad, Robert Gerald, came here for the match races about 1975 in a support race. He was a national club racer but he loved it. He was quite a competitive guy. I used to kick around with a gang of lads who got together on race weekends. My memory of Mallory at that period is that my dad would never get a good result there.

'In later years I got to ride in the British Championships there but even in the early days when I started club racing, again it was not one of my favourites because it was still tough to get a result there. It is challenging. Gerard's is such a unique type of corner. It's one that takes a lot of spirit and confidence. When you are learning your trade and your management are just getting your confidence

From left to right: Jamie Whitham, Terry Ryman, Rob McElnea, Ron Haslam.

up, somewhere like Mallory Park, where you enter into a corner the fastest that you have ever entered into any corner, does take some confidence to get it working right. It's one of those tracks where you needed to do miles there. It was not until I reached a national level that I got comfy riding at Mallory really.

'The hairpin section and, indeed, the Esses is quite similar to lots of circuits that you go to. Gerard's is totally unique. It is 180 degrees – like a fifth-gear hairpin. It is a 180-degrees corner but you are carrying 130mph. It's like a European-type corner in a little English track. For some of the big names who come here and grew up on circuits like this in Europe it is second nature to them. Of all the tracks we go to all round the championship across Britain there is nothing like that at all.

'So you will get the lads who grew up locally and go to Mallory test days every other week who will definitely shine at Mallory and you wouldn't see them go well at other tracks. If they grew up at Cadwell – which is a real all-rounder type of circuit – you could pretty well take yourself everywhere but this was a one-off specialist type of track. Once you eventually crack it and you are at a level where you are at the front at every type of circuit, you can cope with it.

'It was never unchallenging. It was just frustratingly unique that you would get lads that you had never seen before get a result ahead of you and be a pain in the arse in the middle of a season. Then you would go onto your Snettertons and your Brands Hatch and you would be back to normal. Mallory is a thorn in a lot of riders' sides. That said, it was a great place to come to. It was always unique with the characters who went there and what you got back from the circuit. It was very special. It was so different.

'As for Mallory Park as "The Friendly Circuit" – if you haven't been around bikes much, you will find it is like that. There is a lot of camaraderie among the teams and riders. At a national event we still mix with the others and have fun. A lot of people respect that and we like to give a bit back like that. I don't think that it changes from club level right to the top of the sport. That's why I think we have been so popular over the years, even though it has grown over the years and we have surpassed touring cars now. We are still bikes.

'Mallory Park is a really good example of that. The people around the circuit know what Mallory is. It just seems to be at the core at Mallory Park, that type of character – comradeship and getting the job done.

'As for changes – it's the type of circuit, with it being so small and condensed, that that the law of averages says you will attract riders doing forty-plus-second laps. So you will get more silly crashes. That has played against them over the years where the bikes have got quicker and the tyres have got better. That has pushed the barriers further every year. It was getting to the point where the bikes were getting too fast for some parts of the track. So they had to make changes. The Bus Stop was the first that they introduced about a dozen years ago. Now we are doing similar lap times with the Bus Stop, so that has moved

Rob McElnea – number eight.

on. Edwina's was introduced to influence the Esses. It is great that they are all pro-active to keep it safe and look after the riders. There are plans in 2006 for the Gerard's exit to be slowed down. We want to come racing at Mallory Park – it is a unique circuit. The TV people like going there. The crowds love going there and we want to keep going there. It is grand that the circuit owners want to keep attending while listening to what the teams and the riders are saying.

'We are pleased that the new management is so supportive of our sport. We go to practise there and it is cost effective. It is so expensive to turn a wheel on these bikes in the modern era. We do book our own track time and test in Spain. Mallory Park is accessible all the year round. We have to try bikes out but watch the costs. So we will come to Mallory. It is always a good benchmark. We have got good data from there and you know that if you can manage a good lap time then it's quite right and your rider is quite right, mainly the rider. If you can achieve a good lap around there it is mainly down to the rider. It is the bike to a certain degree but it is about being confident.

The start.

The entry to Gerard's.

Gerard's.

Gerard's.

Gerard's exit.

Stebbe Straight.

The approach to Edwina's.

The entry to Edwina's.

Edwina's.

Edwina's exit.

The Esses approach.

The Esses and Oval.

The hairpin approach.

The hairpin entry.

The hairpin.

The Bus Stop approach.

The Bus Stop entry.

The Bus Stop.

The Bus Stop exit.

Devil's Elbow approach.

The Devil's Elbow.

The Devil's Elbow exit.

The finish.

'I ended my career at Mallory Park in a big dusty heap. My teammate James Whitham crashed into me at the Esses. It ruined my golfing for a couple of years!

'I won the British Championship there in 1991 and got thrown into the lake! I did have some great races at Mallory Park and some fantastic ones with James Whitham. At one time he did carve me up at the hairpin. It's a section where you go into a corner and you are off the throttle. Your bikes are quiet and a couple of thousand fans heard me shout every expletive you can imagine at Whitham! They definitely heard me. When I met fans afterwards they were telling me what I had sworn at him!

'Now that I am a team manager I find it difficult being an ex-rider. You feel a lot of reactions compared with a manager who has not ridden. My biggest attribute to the team is that I do get close to the riders and I drag out what they want. Over the years I have had to change a lot in my outlook. It is a huge business now. In excess of a million pounds is required to go racing every year. That's the show we put on now. We enjoy gates of up to 30,000. We have live television. It's a huge sport now. This would have been World Championship level in previous times. The bikes, the back-up, the media coverage – it has all

James Whitham.

James Whitham.

moved on. It could have easily ticked over at the level that it was but a few people got their teeth into it who were enthusiastic and wanted to make it work. I was involved at the very beginning when we first signed with the BBC and have been with it ever since. I would like to think that my Virgin Mobile team and our riders over the years have made a major contribution to it. I enjoy this series. It has been an interesting transition from riding to management. I've had a good time with it. I've had some great guys. I've had some great success. I'm an ex-rider and I really want to be at the front as much as I can but understand how much it takes to get there.

'We always attend the Race of the Year. We like to support Mallory and we know Mark Jessup and John Ward, the new manager. We have items to test on the bike and it's difficult to test in a racing scenario in the middle of the season. So that is a non-championship race and we can try some parts for the bike. So we get a direction as to where we are going to go for the winter testing. We try and get the bike built at Mallory.'

THE LATE AND GREAT

This chapter pays tribute to certain icons of motor sport who had links with Mallory Park in their lifetime and later include those who are commemorated with statues commissioned by Chris Meek.

BARRY SHEENE MBE

Double World Motorcycling Champion Barry Sheene made headlines both on and off the track and attracted a whole new audience to the sport during his 1970s heyday. Controversy and disaster were never far away, with Barry's playboy lifestyle and injuries sustained in several high-speed crashes occupying the front and back pages of the newspapers.

Born in London in 1950, Barry had motor racing in his blood. He was the son of a motorbike engineer and was riding by the age of five. He made his professional debut at eighteen, riding a 125cc Bultaco, and two years later won his first major honour – the British 750cc title. The European title followed in 1973 but, two years later, he suffered his first major crash. In Daytona, Florida, he came off at more than 175mph, breaking his thigh, wrist and collarbone, but incredibly he returned to riding within six weeks. And just one year later he won the first of his two 500cc World Championships for Suzuki, with five wins and a second place. Barry successfully defended his title in 1977 with six wins from nine starts, and his great rivalry with American Kenny Roberts helped draw a huge new audience to the sport.

Between 1975 and 1982, Barry won more international 500cc and 750cc Grand Prix races than any other rider, and he was awarded the MBE in 1978.

However, in 1982 he smashed into a bike lying across the Silverstone track during a British Grand Prix practice. Surgeons rebuilt his shattered legs using metal plates held together by twenty-seven screws. From then on he struggled to find a bike capable of matching his talents and eventually announced his retirement in 1985.

The pain caused by arthritis – brought about by broken bones and exacerbated by Britain's cold climate – prompted him to move to Australia in 1987. In October 2001 he was inducted into the Motorcycle Hall of Fame with a ceremony at Phillip Island, off the coast of Victoria. In 2002 he was diagnosed with cancer of the throat and stomach. Displaying his forthright approach, he vowed to fight it. 'Although this is a complete pain in the arse, it happens to a lot of people and a lot of people get over it,' he said.

Barry may have lost that final battle but, for many, even those who had no interest in motorcycling, he was a national hero.

Maggie Smart, Barry Sheene's sister: 'Our dad was involved in trials and riding bikes himself from when he was a young man. He used to ride at the Isle of Man in the clubman's races. I suppose he came to the fore with his two-stroke knowledge. He was a bit of a two-stroke genius. He did an awful lot of development work for the Bultaco factory in the late 1950s and beyond. With his involvement Barry then had bikes to ride when he wanted to race. The learning curve was also very early for him. Barry used to be in the workshop with Dad from a very early age. He had his own motorcycles as well, for Dad built a little bike called "The Sheene Special", which I've still got. That was a 50cc machine. Barry first sat on a bike when he was just about able to stand up. So throttle control was learnt early.

'Dad used to sponsor riders on his bikes and Barry thought that he could have done a lot better than those riding them. There used to be practice days at Brands Hatch every week. Barry used to hop school and go to Brands. When he was about sixteen he asked Dad, "Why don't you just let me have a go round?" This he did and the rest is history. Barry had his first race at Brands on a 125 and a 250 Bultaco. My father gave Barry 100 per cent support from day one. Barry learnt a lot and was very knowledgeable about how it all worked. If you went into a paddock now there is hardly any rider that is good at spannering as well as riding. Barry had an insight and Scott is the same. It's all in the blood.

'Barry got on very well with the whole Overend family. He always enjoyed going to Mallory Park. Even in later years when he had stopped racing I remember them having Barry there as the star attraction. I had never seen so many people lined up who wanted to meet Barry. It was amazing. He was always accessible and available. When he was at Grand Prix level, he would sit for hours

Barry Sheene leads at Mallory.

on the steps of his motor home signing until the last fan had received their autograph and he had had a chat with them. He was really good at that. Now you go to a Grand Prix and you never see a rider. They all think they are too big now. It is a shame.

'Larger than life is what you would call Edwina. She was the nicest lady and Barry loved her. He always had time for Edwina. She was a lovely lady. Everybody loved Edwina. As for their predecessors at Mallory Park – Motor Circuit Developments – they were not necessarily totally hard-nosed. The guy in charge of the circuits, Chris Lowe, was a super guy. He was always very nicely dressed in a suit and a shirt and a tie. He was friendly. My husband, Paul, got on really well with Chris Lowe.

'In Paul and Barry's era, the depth of British talent meant that the races were pretty fast and furious. The first Transatlantic races were in 1971 and Paul was in those with Triumphs and BSAs. It grew from there. Paul didn't do that many Transatlantics because he raced in America. The Transatlantic series were great. However, by the end of the weekend you were exhausted. On the Friday you did Brands Hatch, which was fine for us. Then on the Saturday you travelled up to Mallory Park to stay near there for the Sunday. As soon as the racing had finished at Mallory Park we were on the road again, up to Oulton Park for the Monday. That was a really hard weekend. It was not just a strain on men and machines

Edwina Overend and Barry Sheene.

but on everything. It was a nightmare by the end of the tour. Then for us there was a 250-mile journey home. They used to get tremendous crowds. Despite all that, the Transatlantic races were great.

'As I revisit the circuits today I am reminded that in those days facilities were very basic. There wasn't any real discussion of safety issues either. We now realise how thin the leathers were that they used to wear. Paul has got leathers back from the 1970s and there is no protection in them at all. Today they have humps and back protectors. They are just so much heavier and thicker. It is a different world.

'Paul's career effectively finished at Mallory Park. Paul and Barry had an incredible race in September 1974 to contest the Race of the Year. With that race over it was the final Superbike race of the day. They were battling for the lead. It was the last lap and you saw them going through the Esses absolutely together, so you didn't know who was going to come out to take the chequered flag. It was Barry and not Paul. Barry took the flag and he went straight back up to the hairpin. Then I knew that something horrible had happened. I had been standing in the pit area. I had to run up the grassy bits to the hairpin. Paul's brake cable had sheared and he had no brakes. Barry had thought, "Christ, Smarty, you're leaving your braking bloody late!" Barry sat up to brake and realised there was a problem. As he looked at Paul, Paul was standing on the footrest trying to brush the speed off. Paul broke both his femurs in the fall.

'Exactly a year before that happened to Paul, Tony Jefferies had crashed at the hairpin and broke his back. That put him in a wheelchair. Ray Pickrell also had a bad accident at Mallory Park in 1972. He smashed his pelvis at the Devil's Elbow. Barry suffered his fair share of injuries but he always remained very outgoing, very vivacious and full of flair. This translated into his motorcycling.

'He always had time for people. He had an amazing ability to remember people's names. He would never ignore people or tell them that he didn't have time – that he was too much of a superstar. As I said earlier he would spend time signing autographs until the last person had got their request. It was also much more sociable between riders than it is now.

'After Barry's accidents he was quite ready to pack up. He had had enough. Also they were planning on children and that influenced him too. He did a bit of car racing and a bit of truck racing. Then he took up television commentary. When he went to Australia he did build up a whole new career with TV work. He had the personality and the Aussies loved the cheeky chappie image.

'Originally he had no desire to go to Australia at all. He used to say that he didn't particularly like Aussies much – that's strange to record now. A friend of his was going and said, "Why don't you come?" Barry wasn't keen but I told him, "Go, you might like it." I regretted saying that for evermore, because he did go and he did like it and he took our parents to live there. He liked the lifestyle but he particularly liked the climate. That's why he moved to Queensland.

'When his health challenge came along, he tried to fight it. Although he didn't want an operation and he didn't want chemotherapy. He wanted to try and do it his way. That was one battle that he lost. Gone but never forgotten. He was a great ambassador for motorcycling. The sport today is because of Barry. He gave it a new profile.'

Paul Smart: 'I knew Barry before he even started racing. I eventually saw him in a different light as the relationship that I had with him was obviously different to the man in the street. These were people who met him after he became successful.

'We went Grand Prix racing together in an old caravan and an old van. We teamed up and went off together. We had a tremendous amount of fun. He was as he appeared. What you saw was what you got. Great fun to be with. A hell of a character.

'I married his sister in 1971 but I had first met Barry when he was trials riding at about twelve years of age. Maggie first came to the circuits with her father

Barry Sheene (7) races Kirk Ballington (34) and Gary Crosby (11) at the Race of the Year, 1981.

and her brother. Her father was a Bultaco importer. Frank was always known as "Franco" because Bultacos came from Spain – General Franco! A fabulous character, Franco, absolutely brilliant.

'Barry was ever so easy to get on with. Obviously everybody has got some downsides. Barry was very self-confident. He was never wrong in his life. None of his decisions were ever wrong. We were at Suzuki together at one time, so we rode side by side a lot. The wonderful thing was that I had great confidence in his riding ability. Barry was very neat and tidy – very easy to ride with.

'We used to go and practise at Brands. We just went out and had fun together. We went once and were jumping up and down because we had broken the track record by a second and a half. All we had been doing was riding around for fun – leaning on each other because we could.'

Scott Smart: 'I used to travel to meetings with Uncle Barry as a kid, so I only ever saw the pits and paddock, plus rubbed shoulders with Grand Prix stars. Not the usual form of spectating! He was very attentive to me as a child. However, he wasn't so keen when I took up his sport but his advice was to the point and welcome. I spent time with him towards the end of his life and our relationship was obviously very close.'

Colin Seeley: 'I have known and dealt with the family for a long time. It was December 1971 that Maggie Sheene married Paul Smart. Barry probably didn't realise at the outset that he would be racing against his brother-in-law. I had always dealt with Frank Sheene – he's a lovely old boy. So I had a long involvement with the Smart/Sheene family anyway.

'Then, in 1971, my direct involvement with Barry came when Suzuki came up with the 500cc Daytona Grand Prix machine. It got ridden in the Isle of Man by Malcolm Uphill. He didn't finish in a race but the bike didn't handle at all. Suzuki GB came to me and said, "Could you make a frame for it?" Another rider took it to the TT and finished third on it with a Seeley frame. It went from there. So then I built some more bikes for them. Eddie Crooks, the Suzuki importer, was bringing the engines in. Then Suzuki came to me to build the 750 version. So in 1973 Barry won the 500cc British Championship and the 750cc European Championships on Seeley-Suzukis. After that we built this monocoque bike. Barry rode that at Mallory Park and was winning on it first time out when it ran out of fuel. We had a bag tank in it and it developed a problem. The relationship with Barry was good from this promising start. For a rider Barry Sheene was mechanically knowledgeable.

'Barry was totally flamboyant. Outgoing, no-nonsense, loved the women. He smoked too much, which probably finished him off at the end of the day. He was a real character and he captured the public imagination – especially his Brut adverts with Henry Cooper. We went through a period when everybody knew Geoff Duke, John Surtees, Mike Hailwood and then Barry Sheene. It was that sort of situation and even today everybody has heard of Barry Sheene. He did a lot of good for his sport.

'He was an extremely good rider and he served his apprenticeship. He rode from 125cc upwards. He rode a great variety of bikes. He almost won the 125 World Championship at his first attempt. Then he went to the TT, didn't like it, and fell off on the first lap. I saw an article in the *Guardian* in mid-2005. It was talking about the TT and really had a go at Barry, saying that his name was rubbish on the island because they thought he wanted to ban the TT. That was not true at all. He didn't. Barry chose not to go there. My wife, Eva, said that I should have contacted the *Guardian* and I didn't. I should have done to get the balance of truth right. Never ever did he say ban the TT. He said, "This is not for me, I don't want to go there." It was Agostini, when a close Italian friend Gilberto Parlotti got killed, who said enough is enough.

'Barry was a very talented rider who had two awful accidents. I was at Daytona when he had his first one. It was suggested that the tyre actually exploded. That's not true. I spoke to Rex Wyatt, who was team manager. Rex is no longer with us. On the highest-speed banking at Daytona with the centrifugal force, the actual tyre expanded to the extent that it locked itself in the swinging arm.

Barry's persona.

'Although overall Barry won two World Championships, he didn't have quite the success that Mike Hailwood had. But he played an enormously important part in his chosen sport.'

JIM CLARK OBE

One of the all-time great Formula One racing drivers. Jim Clark won 25 of his 72 Formula One races and won the World Championship on two occasions in 1963 and 1965, as well as winning the 1965 Indianapolis 500.

Jim drove his entire F1 career for Colin Chapman's Team Lotus. His career total of Grand Prix wins has only been surpassed by five drivers in more than thirty years since. Jackie Stewart, Nigel Mansell, Alain Prost, Ayrton Senna and Michael Schumacher all benefited from a much longer GP season.

1968 started promisingly, with Jim winning the South African Grand Prix in January. However, the year's potential came to an abrupt end during a relatively unimportant Formula Two race at Hockenheim, Germany on 7 April. He had never had a major accident in his career but mysteriously crashed into trees at over 140mph. He was killed instantly.

Sir Jackie Stewart: 'Jim Clark was the greatest ever racer I saw in action or competed against. He was the epitome of a smooth, silky driver. He could take himself and the car to the ultimate limit – but smoothly.

'The relationship between Jim Clark and Colin Chapman was similar to that of myself and Ken Tyrrell. We put all our eggs in one basket and it led to success. However, Colin Chapman could be a controversial figure and Jim was anything but controversial.

'Perhaps Jim didn't enjoy the best of contracts in his career because he was so modest and that is a pity. We were good friends and being Scottish was part of our bond. We shared a flat in London from 1965 to his sad death in 1968. We would not only race each other in the summer months but also in the Tasman series in New Zealand and Australia. So we could continue being pals off the track.

'Jim was such a good person to understudy. He was an immense influence on me and the way I drove.'

The *Hinckley Times* of Thursday 17 April 1997 reported, under the headline 'Flying Scotsman back on track': 'Hands pushed firmly into the pockets of his racing suit, Jim Clark can be seen walking to the entrance of Mallory Park, as though retracing steps he took so often in the early 1960s.

'The life-size statue of the twice World F1 Champion was the idea of circuit owner Chris Meek, a contemporary of the Scotsman and depicts Clark in mid-pace.

'The bronze statue is the work of David Annand, a young sculptor from Kilmany, the village where Clark was born.

'Mr Meek says: "He has captured in every detail the way Jimmy walked as he was a shepherd and had a farmer's gait, and right down to the boxer's boots he always wore. When I was asked to stand next to the statue, it was an eerie feeling as it was so much like him and it gave me goose pimples," added the circuit owner.

'Mr Ian Scott-Walker, entrant for the Border Reivers sports car team for which Clark drove from 1959, was one of those invited to unveil the statue and he recalled the Scot's association with the circuit in the early 1960s: "Jim and I came down here a great deal in the past and looking up my records in the scrap books, I think he probably won more races here than at any other circuit," said the man who was returning to Mallory for the first time in around thirty years.

"I am delighted Chris has taken this initiative. For a long time after his death, out of deference to his family, no-one erected a statue or anything and there was only the Jim Clark Museum at Duns but I know they are very happy this has now happened," said Mr Scott-Walker.

'The other man asked to officiate at the unveiling, Mr Roy Salvadori, who flew in from Monaco specially, was Clark's co-driver when they finished third in the 1960 Le Mans 24-Hour race. "We were teammates for two years in the Aston Martin team. He was always a good driver and just got better and better. He was one of the greatest, possibly the greatest driver who ever lived and a great teammate with tremendous team spirit. I am delighted that there is now a magnificent memorial to him," added Mr Salvadori.

'The occasion was given added poignancy by Mr Carl Wilkinson, Pipe Major of the Royal British Legion, Humberstone, who played Scottish airs and dirges. Mr Meek said: "It was absolutely incredible. As the piper struck up, the sun came out for five minutes, just long enough for the unveiling. It was though Jim had waved a hand and it was very emotional."

The unveiling of the statue for Jim Clark in the presence of the Pipe Major of the Royal British Legion.

COLIN CHAPMAN

Anthony Colin Bruce Chapman was born in 1928 in London. Colin Chapman seems to have been taken by fast machinery from an early age. He learned to fly at university and, after earning a degree in civil engineering in 1948, he was for a short time a flying officer in the RAF.

He became determined to achieve great things as a driver. His approach to covering the financial requirements was to build the car for himself, demonstrate its qualities on a trials course, and then sell innovations and services, and later copies of the cars. He started Lotus Engineering Ltd in 1952 while still working full time. It was tough going after Lotus cars became well known as winners. Colin branched out from trials machines to cars, achieving success at that level as well. At the end of 1954 he quit his day job to devote himself entirely to Lotus Engineering and Team Lotus, the competition arm of the company. Lotus Engineering built both road and competition sports cars, eventually Formula Two and, in 1958, Formula One cars as well.

Although his early cars were based on the space frame chassis, the chassis development that he is most famous for was the full monocoque that he made in the Lotus 25. The 25 was the first of Colin's F1 world-beaters and carried Jim Clark to his first World Championship.

Colin Chapman's story remains half told until Jim Clark is brought into it. Several Lotus drivers won only because they were in a Chapman car. But many Lotuses only won races because Clark was in them. They were an odd couple to say the least, but Colin Chapman was genuinely devastated by Clark's death in 1968 in a Lotus 48 Formula Two car.

Colin was always considered a hardware person and not a people person. Yet some of the greatest names in racing won for him, including Clark, Hill, Rindt, Peterson, Andretti, Mansell and Fittipaldi. After Colin Chapman's death in 1982 and while vestiges of his influence still remained with the team, Ayrton Senna chalked up victories in Lotuses. Such drivers are seldom found consorting with mediocre cars.

Colin Chapman tossed his cap in the air in celebration of an F1 victory for the last time at the Austrian Grand Prix of 1982, which Elios De Angelis took in a close finish from Keke Rosberg. His death from a heart attack in December of that year was shockingly sudden and a surprise to everyone who had followed his unparalleled career.

Chris Meek: 'My first meeting with Colin Chapman was at Goodwood in the late 1950s. He was one of our greatest innovators, with an absolute passion for the sport, a racing driver quicker on the day than the late Jimmy Clark. He was fully capable of aspiring to Formula One World Champion in his own right.

Chris Meek's Radio Luxembourg car.

'It was probably in 1958 that he approached me at Aintree. I was on the second row of the grid in my old Lotus when Colin came up to me, telling me I should be driving one of his new cars and then I would be on the front row. He suggested that I came down to the factory to see him. I didn't take him up on his offer. A year later, when I was able to beat the unbeatable Lotus Elites at Mallory Park in the Elva Courier, I had a call from Colin repeating his offer. By that time I had accepted an offer from Frank Nichols, the boss of Elva Cars Limited.

'It was only in the 1970s that I took his advice and he built a Lotus Europa for me. I told him that I was only interested in outright wins. He said it could be done on our short British circuits. Once again he was right. With Radio Luxembourg sponsorship, wearing 208, I won outright, as he predicted, first time out at Mallory Park. This car went on to win 100 races outright. What might have happened if I had taken his advice in the 1960s? So how could I not honour the great man with a life-size statue at Mallory Park?'

The following press release was issued by the Mallory Park Estate for 18 July 1998: 'At midday on Saturday 18 July a full-size statue of Colin Chapman, founder of the Lotus car company, will be unveiled at Mallory Park by his widow Hazel.

The unveiling of Colin Chapman's statue.

'There is already a full-size statue on the site alongside a large memorial to Team Lotus. The position of Colin's statue means that the tribute to his team will now be flanked on one side by Chapman and on the other side by his favourite driver. The two statues are the work of the well-known sculptor David Annand.

'There have been a number of celebrations to mark the fiftieth anniversary of the founding of the Lotus racing car business but this is the only one to create a permanent memorial to one of the most outstanding car designers of the twentieth century.

'The proceedings will begin with a special tribute to Colin performed by the drivers of the fifty Lotus cars that have been invited to attend.

'Chris Meek will then give his own personal views and memories of Chapman for whom he had, and still has, the finest admiration. Chris spent several seasons racing various Lotus models, winning more events than any other driver in the history of the marque and receiving the coveted Chapman Trophy from Colin no less than three times.'

Above: Lotus achievements.

Left: Chris Meek receives the Chapman Trophy from the man himself.

THE LATE AND GREAT

ROGER CLARK MBE

In January 1999 World Rally Champion Roger Clark, Britain's most successful rally driver of the 1960s and 1970s and local hero, was similarly honoured. He now stands with the other illustrious names. The ceremony was attended by Walter Hayes, latterly vice-chairman, Ford of Europe and the man who inspired the Escort rally car programme, Stuart Turner, Ford's director of motor sport from 1969 to 1975, and by many of Roger's and his wife Judith's friends from the British Racing Drivers' Club.

Roger Albert Clark was born in Narborough, Leicestershire in 1939. He started rallying in 1956 with an old Thames van borrowed from his father's garage. He then moved on to a Renault Dauphine and a Mini. After an inauspicious introduction to the sport at national level in 1961 he was competing at international level by 1963. He drove for Rover from 1964 and this was a successful season for Roger, winning the Scottish and Welsh rallies. He repeated his success in the Scottish rally in 1965 and was second in the Acropolis rally in Greece. Roger joined the Ford works team in 1966. In 1968 he was first in the Circuit of Ireland, the Tulip rally in Holland, the Shell 4000 in Canada and the Acropolis in Greece.

His victory in the 1972 RAC rally, the first by a Briton, propelled him into the national consciousness and this was reinforced when he appeared in a television advertising campaign for Cossack hairspray. He sealed his reputation with his 1976 victory in the RAC – his own initials being most appropriate!

Mallory Park was the base of his development of the four-wheel drive Rallycross Capri alongside his brother Stan. Roger retired in 1987. Besides the statue at Mallory he is now also remembered by the annual Roger Albert Clarke rally, which was launched in 2004.

Chris Meek: 'What can I say about dear Roger that hasn't already been said? I had known Roger for about thirty years and became good friends when I moved into his territory and became his neighbour at Mallory Park.

'The family had adopted Mallory Park as their second home and their hell-raising stunts on speedboats and water-skis became the focal point of the thirteen-acre lake in the centre of the circuit.

'Roger and his wife Judith and their boisterous boys Oliver and Matthew were fun-loving, like their father. Roger was unassuming and during his short life lived it to the full. This is endorsed by his many friends throughout the world, as was his passion for cars, boats and planes.

'Roger's ability as one of the greatest rally drivers needs no endorsement. His name still lives on in the Roger Albert Clark (RAC) Championship. He told me many times how very proud he was being a member of the BRDC and was elated on becoming a director.

The unveiling of the Roger Clark statue.

'Sadly, his loss through illness at such a young age left a gap in the sport that can never be filled. To me Roger is still with us at Mallory Park in the form of a life-size bronze statue in his memory that will live on forever, guarding the entrance to the race circuit.'

MIKE HAILWOOD MBE GM

An obituary from *Autosport* on 26 March 1981 encapsulates the personality and the achievements of Mike Hailwood who, like his mentor John Surtees, enjoyed an amazing career so closely tied with Mallory Park: 'On Monday afternoon came the dreadful news that Mike Hailwood had succumbed to injuries sustained in a road accident at the weekend, which also took the life of his daughter, Michelle. At present the whole world of motor sport is stunned. The precise circumstances of the accident are not yet clear, and indeed are of no real consequence; the fact of the matter is that Mike, winner of countless races and title, survivor of innumerable track accidents, is gone.

'History will remember Mike Hailwood first and foremost as indisputably the greatest racing motorcyclist of all time, the winner of ten World Championships, the man who made the impossible happen. His sheer class and superiority made him a hero across the world. So sure was his touch, so innate his talent, that he was able – after an absence of ten years – to return to the Isle of Man in 1977 and win. He repeated the feat the following year.

'Mike had two stabs at Grand Prix racing, beginning in 1963 with Reg Parnell's private team. For a couple of seasons he was a frequent competitor but there was little chance of success against the factory teams, and by 1965 he had lost interest, returning to motorcycles and further triumphs.

'The second time around was altogether different. The advent of Formula 5000 brought him back. In many ways it was a class of racing ideal for Hailwood. He had never truly enjoyed the underpowered Grand Prix cars of the 1.5-litre era, and a combination of primitive chassis and bags of horsepower brought out all his best fighting qualities.

'And there was something else as well. For Mike, racing – any kind of racing – was something to be enjoyed, rather than endured. Having known the uninhibited, guileless camaraderie of the motorcycle world, he had been ill at ease in the rather more precious enclaves of Formula One. A man totally without any kind of pretension, he found in Grand Prix racing a surfeit of self-important tin gods and hangers-on. Mike was always able to laugh at himself – a rare trait among racing drivers – and had little time for those who took themselves seriously. Of all racing drivers I have ever met, he it was who had the sport's ultimate importance most clearly in perspective. "Have you ever seen," he once said in the Zandvoort paddock, "so many miserable people making half a million quid a year?" And then burst out laughing. He was there to have FUN.

'Hailwood returned to racing cars because he had run out of things to win on two wheels and felt that he had done less than justice to himself at his first attempt. He was very successful in Formula 5000 and revelled in its light-hearted party atmosphere, but there still remained the nagging desire to give Formula One another shot. When John Surtees offered him a drive in the 1971 Italian Grand Prix he took it, and his comeback was spectacular. After qualifying only seventeenth, he had the TS9 in the lead by lap twenty-five, and ran in the lead battle all the way. In a blanket Monza finish he was fourth, a tenth of a second from the front.

'At the same track, a year later, Mike finished second, and this was to be his highest Grand Prix placing. Throughout 1972 he was highly competitive, desperately unfortunate, At Kyalami he had been about to take the lead from Jackie Stewart when the suspension broke. In the International Trophy at Silverstone he had been pushing Emerson Fittipaldi for the lead when the engine blew. But, being Mike, he merely grinned and shrugged away his disappointment. And he did win the European Formula Two Championship that year.

'After another year with Surtees – with whom he got along supremely well; in many ways he was a kindred spirit – Hailwood moved to McLaren to drive the Yardley-backed M23. And his true status emerged now, the white McLaren very often keeping company with the similar car of Emerson Fittipaldi, then at the height of his powers. But at the Nurburgring, running sixth with two laps to go, Hailwood went off the road and suffered severe leg injuries. He recovered well but his Grand Prix career was over. That race was won by Clay Regazzoni, whom Mike had courageously freed from a blazing BRM at Kylami the year before. In recognition of his selfless courage, Hailwood was awarded the George Medal.

'Now, seven years later, he is gone. Although Mike Hailwood was never the virtuoso in cars that he was on motorcycles, we will remember his talent with enormous respect, his sheer bravery with awe. Far more important than his ability to drive racing cars, however, was the affection in which he was held. His mechanics revered him, and he often said that he was far more at home in their company than that of his fellow drivers. As journalists we thought the world of him, not least because he always gave straight answers: if it had been his fault, he said so. And more, he would do it with a smile on his face. He might not have won today, but life would still be worth something. And then he would tell a story, puncture some fragile ego nearby, leave you with helpless laughter. There was never any hope for the pompous as long as Mike Hailwood was around, and that perhaps was his greatest contribution to motor racing. He never lost his sense of proportion.

'It is with desperate sadness that we mourn his passing.'

John Surtees: 'His dad, Stan, made sure that Mike followed my path. Stan competed against my father in sidecars before the Second World War and after. I also raced against Stan and then Stan came along and said, "Ah. We want to borrow your 250 Sportsmax," which I had won everything with in 1955. I wondered, but then lent it to him. They had a very successful South African trip with it. In the end I let them keep it. Then, when I changed to cars, I prepared a number of machines to still ride for myself. These were Nortons. Eventually Mike also had those, mainly the 500 Norton that I had ridden. When I finished with MV they got onto Augusta for Mike to follow me. Stan did a deal with Augusta to get Mike a ride. Then, when I finished with the Lola, of course he got onto Reg Parnell, who had the Lolas at the time, and did some drives in a Lola as well!

'So Mike followed me and drove each of the machines that I had. Then he went on and went back to Honda. He returned to me when he finished with his bikes. At that stage, at least, he had finished with his bikes. Together we won a European Championship with my Formula Two car. Mike and I had a good relationship. We had known each other since we started on the scene. My father had known his father all the way through – so we could enjoy an honest dialogue.

'He came up to me once and said, "John, can't you help me sort out the Honda motorcycle – and sort it out in the same way that you sorted out the MV Agusta?" That was something that was just a topic of conversation at the time. Years later he said that I really should have come and sorted it out. In fact I tested his bike after his death. Honda let me try the bike out – his 500 Honda. This was at Mallory Park and also in Tokyo. I rode it twice. He was right – it did need a little sorting out.

'What was so unfortunate, one of the things that I really regret now in life, is that Team Surtees, the team, and the cars we were building for Formula One, were done on a shoestring. We really were on a limited budget, We were still there – with Mike we nearly won the Italian Grand Prix and we set lap records at the Nurburgring and the Austrian Grand Prix. Then I got what I thought was going to be my big opportunity – my first big sponsor at £100,000. It was big for me at that stage. This was Bang and Olufsen, the hi-fi company. Then they gave me notice that they didn't want me to keep Mike because they wanted the

Mike Hailwood in the Surtees TS15, Mallory Park, March 1973.

John Surtees gets to wear the team gloves on this cold day at Mallory Park.

German market. They were quite happy with the Brazilian driver, however. I had three drivers at the time – Jochen Mass, Carlos Pace and Mike. I had to say to Mike, "We just can't continue." That was something that was sad and it was not good for the team. Even worse was the fact that they ended up not paying, which broke my team and I had to close it. So that was a very sad episode.

'Mike's ability overcame all the advantages his father tried to give him over everybody else. His father, to start with, tried to buy him success. If a bike finished in front he would buy it. But Mike's ability shone through. He actually justified having that sort of equipment, whereas in some cases you have seen it hasn't been. His father was a very dominant force – very forceful. He obviously gave him a wonderful start but then Mike was good enough to have maintained the momentum and perform in his own right. So that was good and he was fine with both bikes and cars. He didn't pretend to be technical or go along and develop things. He just drove and drove but at least he was honest about that. He would give an honest report on what was happening so you could sort it out for him. He wasn't a rider to go to Honda because they would push him to his maximum – the bike would never get better. However, give him a reasonable bike and that was fine.

The unveiling of Mike Hailwood's statue. From left to right: Oliver Hailwood, Pauline Hailwood, Phil Read, Geoff Duke, Chris Meek.

'So Mike was a good, honest trier who didn't give up. He wasn't the most sophisticated performer when it came to technical input or anything like this. He just loved what he was doing. He didn't like the fuss and necessarily the fame that came with it. It was so very, very sad how it all ended – tragic, as his daughter was also lost. Also, in the period before, he had been let down so very badly by those whom he had trusted. People that he had gone into business with had let him down so very badly. It was a sad ending to a great career.'

The *MCN* of 30 July 1997 reported, under the banner of 'Legend honoured': 'Race legend Mike Hailwood's memory will live on forever at Mallory Park, Leics, after a statue in his honour was unveiled by widow Pauline on Saturday. The £20,000 bronze was put up after a phone vote by *MCN* readers.

'Mrs Hailwood said: "Having the statue of Mike at one of his favourite circuits is a great tribute to him, and I am amazed that so many *MCN* readers took the time to vote. I'm very touched and I know that Mike would have been, too."

'Hailwood's son David added: "The statue is very lifelike. Now I know where I get my big nose from!"'

EPILOGUE

The following press release was issued on 12 January 2005: 'BARC Ltd are delighted to announce the purchase of Mallory Park (Motor Sport) Ltd. The acquisition of Mallory Park (Motor Sport) Ltd will entitle the BARC Ltd to full operational rights of the superb Leicestershire circuit. The former pony-trekking site, bought by the late Clive Wormleighton, and converted into a tarmac circuit in the 1950s, has largely retained its original concept and layout – a fast, simple venue that provides spectacular motor racing. Because of this, Mallory Park has seen most of the greatest names in motor sport, either on two or four wheels. Such a great history and the undoubted potential of the venue have made the Leicestershire circuit an obvious choice for the BARC.

'The purchase of Mallory Park will take the club's tally of circuits to three, the BARC running both the Thruxton circuit since the late 1960s and Pembrey since the early 1990s.

'The BARC Ltd had been contemplating purchasing another circuit for some time and to acquire such a prestigious venue is great news for the club.

'There are no plans to make any major changes at Mallory, with all existing circuit activities continuing under the new ownership. With a large amount of updating already having taken place at the circuit, no other major work is planned at the circuit at present.

'BARC'S chief executive Dennis Carter stated: "The acquisition of Mallory Park (Motor Sport) Ltd is a natural step for us as a company, fitting in very well with our existing circuit-based businesses at Thruxton and Pembrey. Mallory Park has been part of the core of British motor sport for many years, under the excellent guidance of the Overend family. Our intentions are certainly not radical and the business will continue very much as before, bringing some of the best of events to the Leicestershire circuit."

'A sentiment that was reciprocated by David Overend, Mallory Park's managing director: "I am delighted that agreement has been reached regarding the future of Mallory Park. My family have been involved with the circuit for over thirty years, since 1984 as day-to-day operators. The decision to move on was not an easy one, but both Ron and I are convinced that Mallory Park will prosper with the BARC and that the circuit's traditions and style will continue under their guidance."'

The fiftieth anniversary logo.

POSTSCRIPT

On 1 March 2006 it was announced that the new corners added to the Mallory Park track through the winter had been officially named and are to be known as Charlie's and Stapleton's.

The first part of the new section is a right-hand turn that runs to the left of the existing track. This will be known as 'Charlie's'. 'Charlie's' has been chosen to celebrate the birth of Chris Meek and wife Svetlana's new baby boy, Charlie Yuri, who was born on Saturday 25 February 2006.

The second section, a double left-hander on the right of the existing track, will be known as 'Stapleton's', after a local village.

Other titles published by Tempus

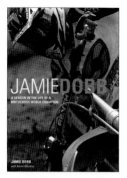

Jamie Dobb A Season in the Life of a Motocross World Champion
JAMIE DOBB WITH ADAM WHEELER

Jamie Dobb is the country's most successful Motocross racer of recent times after becoming Britain's first ever 125cc World Champion at the age of twenty-nine. This action-packed book recounts the twists and turns of his 2002 250cc World Championship campaign as a factory rider with KTM. Offering a fascinating glimpse into the life of a Motocross World champion with all that it entails – fear, crashes, broken bones, excitement, training and gritty determination – this book is an essential read for any Motocross fan.

0 7524 2880 2

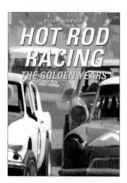

Hot Rod Racing The Golden Years
RICHARD JOHN NEIL

The 1970s saw hot rod racing at the height of its popularity, with large crowds flocking to watch their heroes in action every week. Over the decade the hot rod class moved from being a sport for the working man to one which had professional teams racing in a national Grand Prix series. Captured here in over 200 photographs are the cars, the drivers, the circuits and the events from those golden years of racing.

0 7524 3241 9

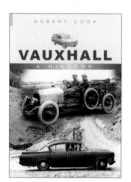

Vauxhall A History
ROBERT COOK

This is the story of Vauxhall, which celebrated its 100th birthday in 2003. From humble beginnings in South London, the company grew to become one of the largest manufacturers of cars in the UK. Written with the help of the Vauxhall archives, this book tells the story of the company from 1903 until the present day. This fascinating history will be of great interest to car and truck enthusiasts as well as local people in Bedfordshire and Merseyside who have worked in the Vauxhall and Bedford plants.

0 7524 3416 0

Minimal Motoring From Cyclecar to Microcar
DAVID THIRLBY

From about 1910 to the mid-1920s, the cyclecar was a popular means of transport. Cheap, simply engineered, often crude, it was really just a motorcycle engine with a lightweight chassis and body. After the Second World War, the Suez crisis also contributed to an upsurge in what were now called microcars. The principle was the same: simple engineering, often with a motorbike engine, in a small package. Inside the pages of *Minimal Motoring* is a history of both the cyclecar and microcar, accompanied by period photographs, advertisements and artwork.

0 7524 2367 3

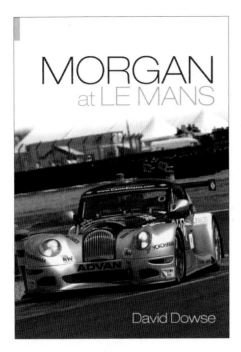

Morgan at Le Mans
DAVID DOWSE

A minnow in a rather large pond – that was Morgan at Le Mans. There they were, one of Britain's smallest car manufacturers, competing with the big boys of Porsche and Ferrari. The story of their Le Mans is one of triumph and tragedy, of David against Goliath. Yet they managed to gain an entry to the world's most exclusive race and, despite their car retiring at the eighteenth hour in 2002, they made a huge impact on the crowds. In 2004 the Morgan Works Team fought its way back to Le Mans – and on to an historic finish that delighted the thousands of fans who had crossed the Channel to support them. David Dowse, then Morgan's press officer and manager of the Morgan Works Race Team, here tells the inside story of an epic battle against the odds.

0 7524 3488 8

Renault F1 1977–1997 Beyond the Yellow Teapot
GARETH ROGERS

The Renault car company's involvement in rallying and other racing competitions entered a new era in 1975 with the founding of Renault Sport. Two years later the first Renault Formula One car was unveiled. With their own team in the years 1977-1985 they had a huge impact on the sport, becoming competitive on the track and revolutionising engine technology by introducing supercharging. Later, after choosing to concentrate their efforts solely on building engines, Renault

achieved remarkable success with the Williams and Benetton teams in the 1990s. There were six consecutive Constructors' World Championship titles from 1992 to 1997 and five Drivers World Championship titles with Nigel Mansell (1993), Alain Prost (1994), Michael Schumacher (1995), Damon Hill (1996) and Jacques Villeneuve (1997). Chronicling this dramatic period, this lavishly illustrated volume tells of the drivers, engineers and other personalities central to the company's success. It recalls great races, on-track rivalries, era-defining technical innovations and more. It is an essential read for any Formula One fan.

0 7524 3553 1

If you are interested in purchasing other books published by Tempus, or in case you have difficulty finding any Tempus books in your local bookshop, you can also place orders directly through our website

www.tempus-publishing.com